Yet I Will Rejoice

International Testimonies of the Lord's Presence

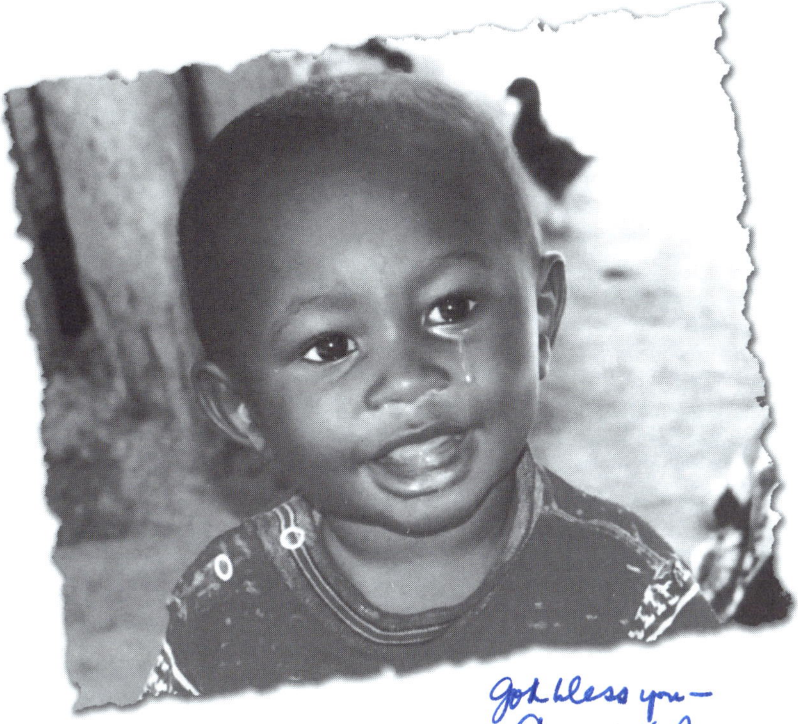

God bless you —
Cheryl J. Barton
Jer. 29:11

Compiled and Edited by Cheryl Johnson Barton

Warner Press
Anderson, Indiana

Copyright © 2008 by Cheryl Johnson Barton. All rights reserved. No part of this publication may be reproduced, stored in a retrieval system, or transmitted in any form or by any means—electronic, mechanical, photocopy, recording or any other—except for brief quotations in printed reviews, without prior written permission of the publisher. For this and all other editorial matters, please contact:

    Coordinator of Publishing & Creative Services
    Church of God Ministries, Inc.
    PO Box 2420
    Anderson, IN 46018-2420
    800-848-2464 • www.chog.org

To purchase additional copies of this book, to inquire about distribution, and for all other sales-related matters, please contact:

    Warner Press, Inc.
    PO Box 2499
    Anderson, IN 46018-2499
    800-741-7721 • www.warnerpress.org

All scripture quotations, unless otherwise indicated, are taken from the HOLY BIBLE, NEW INTERNATIONAL VERSION®. NIV®. Copyright © 1973, 1978, 1984 by International Bible Society. Used by permission of Zondervan. All rights reserved.

Scripture quotations marked KJV are taken from the King James Version of the Bible. Public domain.

Cover and text design by Mary Jaracz
Cover photo by Cheryl Johnson Barton

ISBN-13: 978-1-59317-315-9

Printed in the United States of America.
08 09 10 11 12 13 /EP/ 10 9 8 7 6 5 4 3 2 1

Table of Contents

Introduction 4

Africa
Whether I Live or Die *by Soro Drissa Josue* 6
Why I Serve in Uganda *by Glenna Phippen*. 9
Praise in a Barren Field *by Heather Webb* 12
The Ravager *by Valy Ouattara* 14

Asia–Pacific
A Radical Story *by Eriko Tanaka* .17
The Rascal of Mandalay *by John M. Johnson* 20
Baby Sammy *by Sharon Bernhardt*. 23
Lessons from the Tsunami *by Leaderwell Pohsngap* 26
A New Way Forward *by Song Cheng Hock* 29

Caribbean–Atlantic
Outside the Garden of Eden *by John Ackerman* 32
I Am Not Alone 35
Under a Mango Tree *by Kelvin Harrinarine*. 37
Things You Think but Never Say *by Phil Murphy* 39

Europe–Middle East
A Christmas Perspective *by David and Kathy Simpson*. 43
In the Shepherd's Arms *by Klara Rauleder*. 46
Miracle in Florence *by Susan English*. 49
Sweet Grandma Mary *by Lena Barannikova* 51
I Will Stand and Watch *by Don Deena Johnson* 53

Latin America
The Strong Arms of Christ *by Paul and Brenda Maxfield*. 56
South America on My Heart *by Manuel Killisch* 60
The Battle That Prayer Won *by Luz Gonzales* 63
A Mouth Filled with Laughter *by Noily Hernández* 67
Part of a Plan *by Jon Lambert* 70

Archives
An Angel on Flight 3588 *by Cheryl Johnson Barton* 73

Potpourri
The Fingerprints of God. 77
Behind the Scenes. 88

Yet I Will Rejoice

Though the fig tree does not bud and there are no grapes on the vines, though the olive crop fails and fields produce no food, though there are no sheep in the pen and no cattle in the stalls, YET I WILL REJOICE in the LORD, I will be joyful in God my Savior" (Habakkuk 3:17–18, emphasis added).

INTRODUCTION

Maybe she had never been so afraid in her short lifetime as when the stranger suddenly appeared. Not only had her home been invaded, but the unknown white woman in the infant's mostly ebony world was lurking behind a black camera, coming too close for comfort in preparing to take the photo. The many holes in the little girl's threadbare red shirt, the rough board hut behind her that could not keep out the chicks and other much more worrisome creatures, and the hard-packed, dry dirt ground on which she sat all spoke with exclamation marks of the poverty of Tanzania, her homeland.

There's much one can fear in the world, even one as young as she, pictured on the cover. Not yet speaking or even standing, she certainly had no ability to defend herself against poverty, malnutrition, AIDS and other diseases, genocide and war, and more horrors she knew nothing about—yet. In time, they are likely to become the harsh and unwelcome realities of her life. These too will bring tears.

How different the reaction when her mother appeared! Although a tear still rolled down her tender cheek, a confident smile now lit up her face. From fright to freedom, from tears to triumph—all because she knew her mother. I was still there. So was the poverty and everything else that challenged the daily life of her family. Nothing had changed, except that her mother was now visible. And with her mother's presence, peace, joy, and hope were restored.

What a perfect picture of the way it can be as we relate to our heavenly Father. When we know him, when we understand and believe in the very core of our beings his promise that he is always present with us and will never leave us, we can rejoice no matter what the circumstances. The prophet Habakkuk knew this intimately. It was why, in spite of being so afraid that

Introduction

his heart pounded and his lips quivered (3:16), he declared, "Though the fig tree does not bud and there are no grapes on the vines, though the olive crop fails and the fields produce no food, though there are no sheep in the pen and no cattle in the stalls, *Yet I Will Rejoice* in the LORD, I will be joyful in God my Savior" (Habakkuk 3:17–18, emphasis added).

This is also the testimony of more than 30 missionaries, national church leaders, and lay people in 20 different countries of the world who have written of their experiences in this book, the thirteenth in a series produced by the Global Missions team of Church of God Ministries. Their stories chronicle the pain of domestic violence ("A Mouth Filled with Laughter"), mental and physical illness ("A New Way Forward" and "Outside the Garden of Eden"), war ("The Strong Arms of Christ"), natural disasters ("Lessons from

the Tsunami"), and disillusionment ("Things You Think but Never Say"). Nevertheless, the narratives also are full of praise to God for his love and enduring faithfulness, no matter the trials of life ("I Am Not Alone").

I pray that these stories will encourage and strengthen you in the midst of your own circumstances. May you also testify, *Yet I Will Rejoice!* God bless you.

—**Cheryl Johnson Barton, editor**

Truths that Transform

"'Never will I leave you; never will I forsake you.' So we say with confidence, 'The Lord is my helper; I will not be afraid. What can man do to me?'" (Hebrews 13:5–6).

"Since you are precious and honored in my sight, and because I love you, I will give men in exchange for you, and people in exchange for your life. Do not be afraid, for I am with you. . ." (Isaiah 43:4–5).

"'For I know the plans I have for you,' declares the LORD, 'plans to prosper you and not to harm you, plans to give you hope and a future. Then you will call upon me and come and pray to me, and I will listen to you. You will seek me and find me when you seek me with all your heart. I will be found by you,' declares the LORD, 'and will bring you back from captivity.'" (Jeremiah 29:11–14).

Yet I Will Rejoice

Healed miraculously, he is committed to God…

Whether I Live or Die

by Soro Drissa Josue
(Korhogo, Côte d'Ivoire)

I was born into a Muslim family in 1983 in a small village of northern Cote d'Ivoire. When I was eight, I was sent to live with a maternal uncle, who raised me and provided for my education. I excelled in school and had aspirations of going far in my studies.

However, in the eighth grade, I began having eye trouble. My vision became blurred and I could no longer see writing on the chalkboard. Finally, I had to drop out of school. The local clinic found nothing wrong with my eyes but gave me some medicine. Unfortunately, it didn't help my vision at all. Believing I was the victim of an evil spell, my family consulted witch doctors, Islamic healers, and other false doctors, wasting money and sacrificing animals to appease ancestral spirits on my behalf. But rather than improving, my health continued to worsen.

I fell into depression, having lost all hope of completing my studies. My family sent me to stay with another uncle in the city of Korhogo, but my condition only got worse. I lost all sense of touch and the nerves throughout my body hurt and felt like they were being pulled constantly. Soon I couldn't walk or see.

Just when I thought things couldn't get worse, my whole body began to swell until I couldn't even bend my legs or fingers, and breathing became very difficult. Everything the traditional healers tried only made me worse. My uncle didn't know what else to do but entrust me into the hands of God. He told my family that he'd heard of some Christians who prayed for sick people and that their Lord Jesus healed them. I was filled with joy when my parents told him to do whatever was necessary to keep me alive.

The next day, June 3, 2001, my uncle took me to a place called the Church of God. I remember that day well. It was the day I converted to Christianity and the day that God began to heal my body and spirit. The

The author, Soro Drissa Josue (bottom row, middle), and fellow students in the first class of West Africa Bible Institute, which meets in the building above

church leaders and pastor gathered around to pray for me. Over the next week, my swelling disappeared and my body regained strength, although I was still too weak to walk to church on my own. I felt much better, but my healing was still not complete and my trials were not yet over.

Since my vision remained poor, my uncle sent for a traditional doctor known to heal eyes. Though I was a new Christian and didn't want to return to my old ways, my family pressured me. Because of their taunts, my weak faith, and my desire to go back to school, I reluctantly yielded. However, my vision just got worse. My eyes stung and watered constantly. Then my body began to swell again. My family decided to send me back to the village to be treated by other witch doctors.

The day before I was to return, God intervened again in a miraculous way. Pastor Emmanuel, who'd prayed for me, noticed I'd been absent from church for two weeks. Led by the Holy Spirit, he set out to find me without any idea of where I was. Along the way, he met a woman who brought him to me. Just as I was singing some praise songs I'd learned at church, I looked up and was surprised to see Pastor Emmanuel standing there. He asked me simply, "Do you still want to be a Christian?"

I sincerely did, so he prayed for me and then asked my family if I could stay with his family. That day I came back to the Lord Jesus. Thanks to the prayers of Pastor Emmanuel's family, my health recovered until I could walk to church on my own. I then understood the Devil's tricks to deceive me and made a firm resolution to trust God fully whether I live or die.

I continued growing in faith and strength until I could work in the family fields again. As my eyes improved, I also began studying God's Word. Whenever my health was attacked, I asked the pastor to pray for me and I recovered. However, once when he was on a trip, I became totally paralyzed and could eat nothing. I lost my hearing, except for a voice in my head constantly yelling my name. When my uncle found me like this, he insisted on taking me back to the village. I didn't want to go and prayed for God to intervene. I asked my uncle to let me see the pastor before going. At first he refused, but later he allowed us to stop at the church on the way. Pastor Emmanuel again invited me to stay with his family. They prayed for me day and night, and God delivered me from my illness and from the voice in my head. Each day, I studied the Bible with the pastor, which gave me spiritual strength as well. One month later, I returned home confident I would be able to walk to church and hold firm in my faith. My family was amazed to see me alive and healthy, so the name of the Lord was highly honored among all who knew me.

Even though I'm occasionally sick, I know God has delivered me miraculously and will continue to touch and heal me. I've been diagnosed with high blood pressure and given medicine that has helped me too. My pastor has also gone with me to my village to help me share my faith with my family and find fellowship with other Christians there. He taught me that wherever I go, I can know that my Lord is there with me. Later, I spent eight months in the village. I prayed and studied the Bible daily with other Christians, which fortified my faith and my witness to others, including my family.

I have found strength to resist temptation and walk firmly in God's power. I want to spend the rest of my life serving God for all he has done for me. This is why I am in my first year at West Africa Bible Institute, preparing for the ministry.

AFRICA

Boiling water had seared her tender skin.

Why I Serve in Uganda

by Glenna Phippen
(Kampala, Uganda)

The longer I'm a medical missionary in Uganda, the more I realize I must rely completely on God to help me every minute of the day. Medical missions encompasses so much more than administering medications, applying dressings, and delivering babies. No matter how experienced I may be, working in this environment tests me in every way—medically, physically, and spiritually.

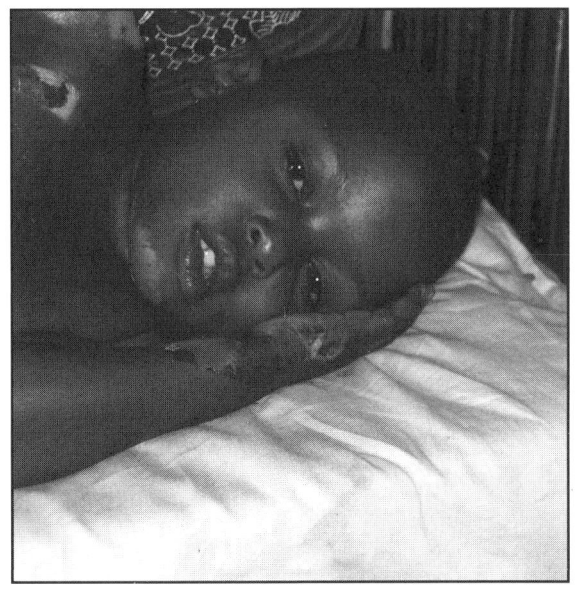

Eveline, four days after her near-fatal accident

One of the most rewarding aspects of my work is freedom, freedom to pray with patients, to share my faith, to talk about trusting God. In fact, it's almost expected. Ugandans are so open to the gospel that they don't think I'm fanatical to talk about Jesus and his power to save and heal. Several times, I've experienced immediate answers to prayer for a sick patient. This is not just a display of God's power, but a genuine expression of his love.

During weekly clinic visits, I make rounds with nursing staff, reviewing each patient's case. I also ask patients and family members if I may pray with them. Not a single person has ever refused.

Yet I Will Rejoice

Glenna Phippen on a home visit in rural Uganda

Just last week, I prayed with a five-year-old and her parents. Burns covered about 30 percent of little Eveline's body. Young as she was, she'd been helping with the cooking, something expected of even little girls here in Uganda. As she tried to lift the kettle from the fire, she dropped it and the boiling water had seared her tender skin. Neighbors helped pay for a *boda-boda* (motorcycle) to bring her the six kilometers to our health center. I was happy they hadn't applied a typical home remedy instead, such as smearing the burns with cow dung. Proper care had been administered quickly by our skilled staff that treats many similar burn cases.

Nevertheless, when I first saw Eveline's listless body just four days after the accident, I was afraid she'd die from infection because of the large surface area of the burns. I'd have expected her to be screaming and crying with pain, but she was just lying there motionless in the crib.

After praying with the family, I taught Eveline and her parents some simple physical therapy exercises to prevent her burned right hand from contracting. Amazingly, when I returned one week later, Eveline was out of bed and playing with her sister. When she ran over to show me how she could do the exercises I'd taught her, I saw a marked improvement in her condition. Although she has some scarring, most of it can be covered by clothing, and her long-term prognosis is very good.

Another blessing is working, sharing, and praying with staff members. At each clinic, I lead devotions with the staff, encouraging them to show Christ's love to our patients. We strive to offer more than just basic medical care. Our goal is that patients know we are different from other clinics because of Christ's love.

After working in the secular arena throughout my nursing career, I'd thought that nursing in a Christian organization would be a glorious, spiritual experience all the time. Now, at the start of my second term, I'm wiser and perhaps more cynical. I've come to realize that we humans are basically the same, with problems and stresses in our lives no matter what our culture or country. My desire—that people will know the love of Christ through everything I say and do—is often put to the test. I'm frequently overwhelmed by all the needs around me and many times feel powerless to help. My idealism is tempered by daily doses of reality where very little shocks or surprises me anymore, although I'm saddened and outraged at the treatment of women and children and completely disgusted with the ever-present corruption. My honeymoon is over.

Nevertheless, I'm encouraged by the warmth and kindness of the many Ugandans who carry on in the face of such overwhelming needs as abject poverty and HIV/AIDS. I want to remember that I am privileged to be the hands and feet of Jesus to them. It is an awesome and humbling task, but when I surrender to God, he takes what I have, adds his power, and does his work. It is not a cliché to say that it's not about me, but all about him. This is why I serve in Uganda.

> *I was afraid she'd die from infection because of the large surface area of the burns.*

This story originally appeared in a shorter form in Missions *magazine, July/August 2006.*

Yet I Will Rejoice

How could God's good plan hurt so much?

Praise in a Barren Field

by Heather Webb
(Dodoma, Tanzania)

The doctor walks into the examination room and shakes our hands. My heart is beating wildly in my chest in anticipation of the news.

"I'm afraid I don't have good news," he says slowly. I stop listening to what he is saying and only hear this one sentence repeated over and over again in my head. Tears well up in my eyes and start spilling uncontrollably down my cheeks. I glance at my husband and see the pain in his face too. The thin paper gown I'm wearing only increases the feeling of vulnerability of having my heart laid bare in front of a doctor and nurse I hardly know.

Usually when a doctor utters this phrase, it's because he's found something: cancer, a tumor, an infection. But in our case, it's because he's found nothing. The pregnancy test is negative. It's not the first time we've gotten this news. In fact, I've lost track of how many times the answer has been no.

The ride home from the doctor's office is quiet and tear-filled. My first response is anger, disappointment, confusion, and gut-wrenching pain. I take little comfort in the promises of Scripture: "All things work together for good" and "I know the plans I have for you."* I am so focused on the pain. It engulfs me and I begin to doubt that any of God's promises are true. It just doesn't seem possible that this could be God's good plan for me. How could God's good plan hurt so much?

Over the following weeks, I pursued God in the midst of the pain. In doing so, I rediscovered an amazing thing he'd taught me before. Even in the midst of difficulty and disappointment, he is still worthy of praise. A prophet says it this way: "Though the fig tree does not bud and

---

* Romans 8:28 (KJV) and Jeremiah 29:11 (NIV).

Africa

there are no grapes on the vines, though the olive crop fails and the fields produce no food, though there are no sheep in the pen and no cattle in the stalls, yet I will rejoice in the LORD, I will be joyful in God my Savior" (Habakkuk 3:17–18).

When my heart is totally engulfed in pain, it's as if I'm sitting in the middle of the barren vineyard surrounded by dried up grape vines with no fruit. My heart is so downcast I can only see the wasteland. This isn't the kind of field I've always dreamed of. All those around mine are bursting with fruit. All I can do is weep in the dirt.

But the Lord of the harvest gently beckons me to focus my attention on him. When I can lift my eyes and my heart from the barren fields to the one who is in total control of my harvest, to the one who can see past this season of drought to a season of beauty and fruitfulness, my heart is indeed comforted. He reminds me of his vast love for me and that he himself created this field and that he didn't make a mistake. He reminds me that he has a good plan even in the midst of a fruitless season. I don't know what will come of this barren field, if it will ever produce fruit, but because of God's promises to me, I can stand in the middle of a barren field with my arms raised high and praise him.

Mike and Heather Webb and their Tanzanian family

Yet I Will Rejoice

One by one, his family was dying.

THE RAVAGER

by Valy Ouattara
(Korhogo, Côte d'Ivoire)

Valy and some of his family

I was desperate. My situation demanded immediate intervention, but I could find no help, until…

My story goes back to 2001 when I often felt sick. My illness—whatever it was—had progressed so much by 2002 that I was in one crisis after another. I even visited three villages seeking traditional treatments. In 2004, my health improved, but oddly enough, my seven-month-old daughter became ill and died. Her death so affected her mother that she too became sick. One week later, I succumbed to my illness and went into a coma. I learned later that my extended family did not think it would be worth it to take me to a hospital. At the same time, they transferred my sick wife to my father's residence, where she died a week later.

A month passed before I awoke from my coma. It was then that I learned of my wife's death. I had another relapse but managed to get from my home in Korhogo, in the north, to the coastal city of Abidjan, in the south, where I could have some medical exams. The doctor did not tell me the results but ordered me to have a scan. I didn't have money for this, so I returned home in early 2005.

A few months later, a friend took me to a clinic in the French military camp. The doctor examined me, took my blood, and told me I was HIV positive. He advised me to get a second opinion at the government hospital, which I did, but the outcome was the same. I had AIDS. It felt as if a cleaver had been dropped on me as the reality of my situation penetrated my mind and heart. It was unbearable news for my family, and my parents and siblings all rejected me.

But I couldn't just lie down and die. I had to concentrate on caring for my two wives and 13 children.[*] Then we found out that my wives are also HIV positive. In February 2006, one of them, one of the children, and I all became ill, and we were hospitalized. A doctor ran further tests on me and found tumors on my liver. I couldn't believe it when he gave me four months to live.

During this very difficult time, my five-year-old daughter died. My friend Gnenema came to console me and suggested contacting his pastor, so I agreed. Together they told me about God and his almighty power. As I hesitated, a battle raged within me between Satan and the word of God they were presenting to me, but I finally chose God. I know I would have regretted it all my life if I'd chosen to continue on Satan's path. Thereupon, my family and I began removing all the fetishes I had placed throughout our house and yard for protection from evil spirits and for healing. I placed everything in a plastic bag and gave it to Gnenema so the pastor could burn them.

One evening I decided to speak to a neighborhood woman who protects our traditions. She was alarmed that I would destroy my fetishes.

---

[*] Missionary Kay Critser, who translated this testimony from French, notes that the traditional practice of polygamy remains prevalent in Côte d'Ivoire today. She says, "Evangelical churches do not allow converted polygamists to serve in leadership. Some have had new converts send away multiple wives and remain with the first. But those sent away can never marry again, and their parents do not want them to come home because of the financial burden. These women often become common to any man who comes along, so polygamy is a major challenge to the church."

I was challenging the traditional teachings and practices I had kept since childhood. I reassured her that in the presence of the Lord Jesus, nothing could cause us to be afraid. God alone will provide for our needs and my health.

I became a member of God's family by being firmly convinced that salvation is found only in Jesus Christ. God then answered my prayers by placing his powerful hand upon the hearts of my wives and children, who also became believers. Our lives have changed for the better. Sickness is rare in our home, and we have peace in our hearts and sense a communion we did not have before.

What remains for me to do now is to pray that God increases my faith, deters me from temptation, keeps me pure, and helps me persevere in love. I rejoice that Christ has done so many wonderful things for my family and me. We have been saved from the ravager of body and soul. We have been given eternal life. Amen!

Death Has No Sting!
by Colleen Stevenson (Kampala, Uganda)

Often we are faced head on with circumstances that suffocate us with heaviness from encountering continual loss. In TAPP, our AIDS program, we see many hopeless situations where there is no one to assist children in the struggle for medicine, food, shelter, and school fees, and in their loneliness from abandonment. After a day of visitations, we were feeling very sad. Then shocking news came that one of our sponsor children, who had just finished his technical training, had dropped dead! Returning home, we saw a teenager hit and driven over by a taxi. It was almost too much to bear.

Many people live with the knowledge that they will soon die. I thank God that we have confidence that death has no sting. Jesus, through his death, conquered death for us. Though we see much death around us, through the TAPP program we are also witnessing many come to Christ. For these, death is overcome. That's why we're rejoicing.

Asia–Pacific

Almost too good to be true…

A Radical Story

by Eriko Tanaka
(Tokyo, Japan)

A blank stare. Until recently, that's how I would have responded if you'd asked what I thought about God. Not to be rude, but at nearly 30 years old, I had no idea about God and no belief that he might actually exist, so I could only have stared blankly. Now, a short two months later, I can't imagine life without him. This is a radical story almost too good to be true. But I hope you will believe it because it has changed my life.

Missionary Bernie Barton baptizing Eriko Tanaka

As I was sleeping in my room on the night of April 26, 2007, I suddenly began bleeding internally. I was totally unaware of what was happening, but my mother and brother say I was throwing up into a plastic trash can and wiping blood from my nose and mouth. Then I rolled up my soiled sheets and pajamas and placed them at the head of my bed. Faintly, I seem to recall the vomiting and diarrhea, but I cannot remember my family trying to get me to respond to them. Worried, they called several hospitals, but it was a holiday week and I couldn't be moved easily.

I continued like that until April 30, my birthday, when my father, who had died of cancer three years earlier, appeared to me—along with Jesus. Because I'd never believed in God or even thought about him, I can't explain how I knew it was Jesus with my father. I didn't see or hear him, but I felt him clearly in my heart and recognized him as easily as if I'd always known him.

Then my bleeding stopped. It was the morning of May 1. Suddenly I felt like going to church, something I'd never done before. I now realize Jesus was leading me there.

On May 3, I finally could walk well enough to go out, so my mother went with me to a nearby church. Then I recalled the location of another church, and we also went there. As I stood before Hagiyama Church of God, I saw its telephone number on the signboard. The last four digits were 0-4-3-0: April 30, my birth date. I knew immediately this was the place I was seeking and began attending services there the very next Sunday, May 6.

> *Though a woman, I wasn't womanly; though human, I didn't live humanly.*

Perhaps you wouldn't believe my earlier life. Though a woman, I wasn't womanlike; though human, I didn't live humanly. Instead, I was a wild teenager who had then lost herself in her twenties after marrying and divorcing. Even now, my wrists bear scars from efforts to kill myself. I visited psychiatrists and took many antidepressants, then sedatives, and almost succeeded the second time I attempted suicide.

Before I met Jesus, I didn't want to get up in the mornings, even though I suffered through the nights with nightmares and terror. For seven years, I slept with lights on because I was afraid of the dark. Mornings were worse. I didn't wash my face. I didn't want to meet or talk to anyone, go out, or use my cell phone. I just wanted to sleep all day long and, if possible, die in my sleep. I was a lost soul, as good as dead. Actually, I was dead; only my body was alive.

But since then, my life has changed 180 degrees. Now I sleep peacefully without lights until morning. When I do awaken, it is not with an alarm clock but with rejoicing in my heart. I'm finally alive as I never was during all the years I wanted to die. Every day as I wake up, I hear the birds singing and am eager to go outside. I love taking a bath and meeting people. It is so wonderful doing simple everyday things that mean you really are alive.

After her baptism, Eriko Tanaka bows and receives flowers from Pastor Ogata.

I doubt I could believe someone who said she saw God in a dream or vision, even if it was someone I trusted completely. But that is my experience. The fact that the living Christ is God and Savior was made clear to me, and there is no changing fact.

Yet sometimes even I wonder if I'm living a beautiful dream. I slap my cheeks and check the calendar to be sure it's true. I can't find words to express my joy and amazement at what has happened to me.

I received a New Testament at the church and read it through twice in two weeks. As my parched soul was filled, I couldn't stop crying. I was asked, "What do you want to be prayed for?" I responded simply, "For my soul to be set free." My prayers have been answered.

The reality of what has happened to me—this radical change—can only be explained by salvation through Jesus Christ, the Son of the all-powerful, all-knowing, ever-loving God. I gratefully give him the rest of my life and pledge to follow him forever.

Yet I Will Rejoice

When his land sold miraculously, he believed.

The Rascal of Mandalay

by John M. Johnson
(Portland, Oregon)

With a population of six and a half million people, the northern city of Mandalay is Myanmar's second largest metropolis. It is also the center of the nation's spiritual and cultural heartland. In March 2006, while in Mandalay, I had the opportunity to visit two different churches. The first one was built around 1900 to honor the ministry of Adoniram Judson, the first missionary to what was then called Burma. The church is built near the site of a royal prison where Adoniram was confined because of his missionary endeavors.

The second building visited was the Church of God. It is one of only 11 Christian churches in the huge city and the only one able to hold services continuously; the others all experience opposition from Buddhist ward captains across the city.* Considering that more than half of all Buddhist monks in Myanmar live in the Mandalay area, it is not surprising that the city is a hotbed of persecution for Christians. Shortly before I arrived, five pastors had been arrested in Mandalay, two of whom were still imprisoned.

What did surprise me was to learn that the Church of God pastor had not been forced to stop his congregation from gathering for worship, despite the growing hostility. When I asked how that was possible, Pastor Naugh Naugh introduced me to a man named Kyaw Thi Ha. Together they told me an incredible story.

Kyaw Thi Ha was the son of a rather wealthy family. This led the Buddhist monk in that area to "invite" him to repair and refurbish the local temple. Kyaw Thi Ha knew that only "worthy" people are approached to perform such service, so he was pleased by this attention. Wanting to gain merit for the next life, he paid to have the temple restored and seven new Buddhist images installed.

---
* Ward captains are the presidents of city district councils.

Asia–Pacific

Pastor Naugh Naugh (left), Kyaw Thi Ha (right) and his wife

Kyaw Thi Ha explained, "Buying images and repairing the temple cost me a lot of money, so I thought I would feel something good as a result. But afterwards I only felt empty inside, emptier than before. I felt like I was missing something, so I resorted to drinking and all sorts of wickedness."

Disillusioned, Kyaw Thi Ha was in and out of trouble. He mistreated his wife and cared little for his children. With the help a translator, Pastor Naugh Naugh explained, "Kyaw Thi Ha was a real rascal." It was at this point in his troubled life that Kyaw Thi Ha heard the gospel through Pastor Naugh Naugh's wife.

"I saw people praying and wondered if their prayers really worked," he recalled. "I wondered if there was a God who really answers prayers. I had a plot of land I wanted to sell but couldn't. I had performed many religious rituals on the property in order to sell it, but nothing had happened. So I asked Pastor Naugh Naugh to pray. He said he would and that the land would sell in three days. I told my wife that if this happened, she must let me become a Christian and go to church with me.

With a large smile on his face, Kyaw Thi Ha continued, "At 6:30 on the evening of the third day, the sale of my land was completed."

True to his word, Kyaw Thi Ha accepted Christ, and so did his wife. They were discipled by Pastor Naugh Naugh and his wife, and subsequently were baptized. The rascal of Mandalay died and the disciple of Christ was born—a transformation so miraculous that it was evident to all, including Kyaw Thi Ha's father-in-law and mother-in-law, who also accepted Christ. Kyaw Thi Ha, the man who had mistreated his family, had become a loving father and husband.

"Only a living Savior could do such a thing," reasoned the father-in-law, explaining why he also accepted Christ.

And who is Kyaw Thi Ha's father-in-law? He is the local ward captain, the very man who is able to keep Pastor Naugh Naugh out of prison.

A Beautiful Harvest
by Zonia Mitchell (Saga, Japan)

During a three-day trip to China, my assignment from Saga University was "to introduce Japanese culture to Chinese students in English." The highlight of my visit was visiting O-ping and her family and reminiscing about the precious memories we made together when they were students in Japan and attended Saga University's Bible study. O-ping excitedly told me how she'd discovered her Chinese English teacher is a Christian and how she encouraged him to start a Bible study on campus. Then she added, "Remember that cloth book about the birth of Jesus that your mother made for my son? He had a school assignment to write about his favorite thing, and he chose that. He reads it in English and has translated and memorized it in Chinese!"

Obviously, seeds planted several years ago in Japan are taking root, growing, and producing beautiful, delicious fruit in China. Thank you for your prayers. They are making a marvelous difference in both Japan and China.

As I held the perfect little boy, my heart broke.

Baby Sammy

by Sharon Bernhardt
(Southeast Asia)

The world is teeming with people. My eyes have glimpsed hundreds of thousands of faces in my short lifetime, yet most are strangers to me. It is hard for me to fathom that God knows each one just as he knows me. When I have the opportunity to see how deeply he cares for each person he has created, I in turn learn even more about the nature of our compassionate Lord.

In October 2006, I got a phone call from a friend. We were making arrangements to have lunch together when she told me that she had a one-day-old baby at her home. He had just been born to a distant relative, and she invited me to come see him. The baby's father was unemployed, and he and his wife already had one child. They felt they could not care for the baby because of their financial situation and were hoping their relative could find a place for him.

As I held the perfect little boy in my arms, my heart broke. He was sleeping so peacefully. He had no concept of the cruelty of the world nor understanding that his parents were planning to leave him. Surely his mother loved him deep in her heart, but she was not holding or nursing him, and had him sleeping in the other room. I was sure she was distancing herself from him. As for the father, there was no emotion or involvement on his part at all. He barely seemed to be present.

Observing this scene, I cuddled the baby even more closely as I thought sadly, "He doesn't even know that no one loves him." Oh, how wrong I was!

I got a call the very next day that the parents were leaving town soon. Could I care for the baby for a while that day and think of anyone who might be interested in adopting him? I immediately began making phone calls, thinking it would be best if he was placed directly into the loving arms of new parents instead of being bounced from home to home.

I called a colleague from school, having heard that her brother might be interested in adopting. She said they were, but added that they were planning to start the process in a year. Still, she promised to contact them.

A few minutes later, one of her other brothers phoned to ask about the baby. He said that just two days before, the brother interested in adoption had come to him and requested prayer because they planned to start looking into the process. Goosebumps covered my arms as I said, "This child was born two days ago!"

> *I felt a reassuring peace since I knew God had orchestrated this.*

Within two hours, the couple that had begun praying about adoption was at my home. Their nervousness was obvious. Would they be holding a baby shortly, or would there be heartache if the birth parents decided to keep him? When the birth parents arrived, I went to the car and took the precious bundle from his mother's arms. She was overcome with sadness, but I did not know what to say. There was nothing to say. Tearfully, she said goodbye to the baby and I carried him inside. There, tears flowed again as the perfect infant was placed into the arms of a couple that had desired a child for years.

There was tension and uncertainty as the couple waited for the adoption paperwork to be processed. They were concerned that the birth parents might change their minds. But I felt a reassuring peace since I knew that God had orchestrated this. What connections he made by using us! We had not known either set of parents before this event. I was confident this baby was born at this time for this particular couple. (One way this was demonstrated was that the paperwork went through smoothly and quickly, even though the families were of different religions—a barrier to adoption in this country.)

The new parents joyfully named the little boy Samuel because of 1 Samuel 1:20, "So in the course of time Hannah conceived and gave

Asia–Pacific

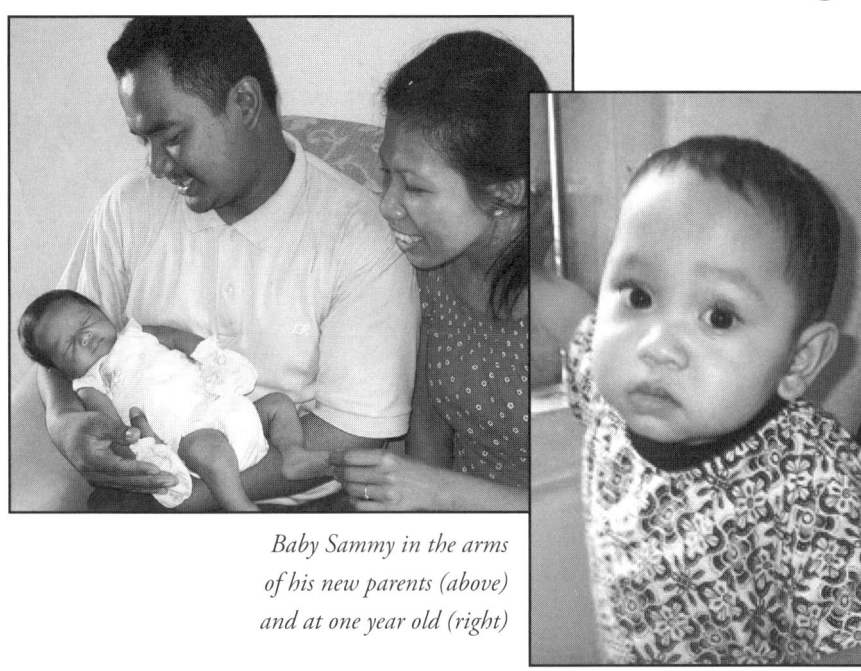

Baby Sammy in the arms of his new parents (above) and at one year old (right)

birth to a son. She named him Samuel, saying, 'Because I asked the Lord for him.'"

Sammy's parents pastor the church we now attend. We have seen how it was in God's plan for us to attend this church—yet another result of this incredible event. We have the privilege of seeing Sammy grow and change. We are able to witness how his life is filled with love as he is raised with the knowledge of Christ. It is a great privilege for us.

I am also reminded that I was wrong when I first met Sammy. Although he did not have parents who could love him that day, he was not unloved. To the contrary, he was loved in a very intimate way by his Creator, who had a plan for him. God had his hand on baby Sammy then, and it is exciting to think about how God will use his life in the future.

Needless to say, Sammy's parents are also full of expectation as they look at the son God gave them and quote 1 Samuel 1:27–28, "I prayed for this child, and the Lord has granted me what I asked of him. So now I give him to the Lord. For his whole life he will be given over to the Lord."

Yet I Will Rejoice

*Unstoppable tears, unending debris,
unanswered questions, and...*

Lessons from the Tsunami

by Leaderwell Pohsngap
(Shillong, Meghalaya, India)

Pain, poverty, and despair. I've seen plenty of it during my lifelong ministry in the Church of God. But nothing compares to what I experienced in South India not long after the disastrous Asian tsunami hit on December 26, 2004. Then chairman of the board of World Vision India, I was expected to go and see the destruction since World Vision was the first organization to respond with relief supplies. I could hardly believe what I was seeing as I struggled to make sense of the horrific destruction all around.

The line of survivors queued to receive relief supplies was long, and the hot sun was beating down unmercifully on their heads. Our people were up on a truck handing down the supplies to those standing

Young boys survey tsunami destruction in South India.

barefooted below on the hot sandy ground. All around, we could still see the shattered houses and boats of the people whose livelihoods had come from fishing. That livelihood was now shattered as well.

When I completed my assigned task, I walked around and talked to people. One family, a grandmother and daughter, had lost a child. I asked them whether they were satisfied with the relief supplies. They nodded their heads slightly, but again and again mourned loudly, "Our child is not coming back." Their grief burned in my heart. I felt hopeless and helpless as I tried to understand their experience.

Witnessing the loss of lives—more than 12,400 in South India alone, not including the 5,640 missing people who were never accounted for—and hearing the stories of some of the nearly 650,000 displaced South Indians living amid unstoppable tears and unending debris was indeed heart-wrenching.* I could not fathom the pain they had endured. How long will it take for them to rebuild their habitat was an obvious question. But there were even deeper questions. Will they ever make sense of the loss? Will they ever forget or be comforted? Will there ever be any healing?

Even as a Christian believer, I had no answers. And there in South India, with its predominantly Hindu population, most of the victims were not believers anyhow. I went home with a heavy heart and a prayer that somehow our being there would help them.

I returned to South India on March 29, 2007, more than two years after the tsunami pounded Indonesia, Thailand, India, and Sri Lanka. This time, I was there with the president of World Vision International for the joyous task of handing over 5,861 permanent houses built by World Vision for some of the South Indian survivors.

I saw an amazing transformation, a world of difference between my two visits. Besides constructing permanent housing, World Vision had also helped create schools and playgrounds for children, meeting halls and counseling centers for communities, and small businesses. I witnessed smiles of people whose lives seemed full of hope again.

---

* In addition to statistics provided for this story by World Vision India, the United Nations reports a total of 229,866 people lost, including 186,983 dead and 42,883 missing, in the four nations most affected by the tsunami (Indonesia, Thailand, India, and Sri Lanka), termed the ninth deadliest natural disaster in modern history.

Yet I Will Rejoice

As we went from one community to the other, cutting ribbons to inaugurate new houses and facilities, the people expressed their gratefulness to us with flowers and words of praise. Those of us from World Vision gave thanks to God. We knew it was his grace that had enabled us to accomplish everything.

Housing constructed by World Vision

Entering one house already occupied by an elderly lady, we found the walls bare except for one picture of Jesus. "Are you a Christian?" we asked her. "No," she answered, "but I love Jesus Christ." Her answer made me realize that she had already begun her journey towards our God of grace. But how did she know about Jesus Christ?

The World Vision staff is comprised of people of faith, sacrifice, and prayer. For more than two years, as they labored with loving care among many non-Christians, those they helped—including this elderly lady—called them "Jesus people" because their love reflected the love of Jesus. In turn, this attracted others to love Jesus, even though they might not yet know him as their only savior. As a result, many Christian churches have been started in this area.

What lessons do I glean from this experience? There are many. I realize that the God of grace is at work in the very most difficult places and circumstances. Because of this, I can have hope even when I do not understand the situations around me since I know God is at work. This truth challenges me to be faithful because that is all God requires of me; I can leave the results to him. It also encourages me to rejoice even when I see no obvious immediate results because I know God is working nonetheless.

Reflecting upon these lessons from the tsunami, the words of Habakkuk 3:17–18 finally make sense to me: "Though the fig tree does not bud and there are no grapes on the vines, though the olive crop fails and the fields produce no food, though there are no sheep in the pen and no cattle in the stalls, yet I will rejoice in the Lord, I will be joyful in God my Savior."

ASIA–PACIFIC

The psychiatrist's words sounded like a death knell.

A New Way Forward

by Song Cheng Hock
(Singapore)

"The pastor has burned out!"

Honestly, I dreaded that kind of speculation. But what else could people conclude? The symptoms were so evident: I broke down easily and became unusually uncommunicative, moody, and highly sensitive. I wasn't exactly the greatest company to be with. I felt like a failure and was ridden with guilt and shame. For days, I wrestled with a whole gamut of what-ifs, if-onlys, and other regretful shoulds and oughts. I chided myself even as I tried to take comfort in my pastoral calling. How could I be so careless? How could I not see it coming? Why didn't I pace myself? But self-blame only served to deepen my despondency. That was in early 2002.

It was a far cry from the optimism of 1984 when I started my theological training. Then, Joshua's final challenge to Israel sounded unremittingly arresting: "But if serving the Lord seems undesirable to you, then choose for yourselves this day whom you will serve…" (Joshua 24:15). I found that welcoming and irresistible. I chose the obvious—to serve the Lord.

I was realistic enough to appreciate that no vocation is ever frustration free. Admittedly, there were times when I felt discouraged and even considered quitting. But those were just isolated, exasperated, knee-jerk reactions rather than recurring preoccupations. Overall, ministry was satisfying, fulfilling, and meaningful.

But that changed when I found myself increasingly withdrawn and morbidly introspective. I contemplated suicide as frequently as I experienced uncontrollable, rapid-fire thoughts and violent mood swings. I needed little sleep and was extremely energetic, cycling between 70 and 90 kilometers each day (approximately 44 to 56 miles). After much persuasion from my church leaders, I reluctantly consulted a psychiatrist.

"You have bipolar mood disorder," the psychiatrist nonchalantly revealed as though it was a common cold. But it sounded like a death knell to me. I wasn't prepared to carry a psychiatric label. Deep down I was scared. Our shame-accented culture holds many unhappy stereotypes of the mentally ill. At that moment, I wished my friends were correct—that I had just burned out.

My life was in disarray. I was confused and doubted my calling. Did I merely respond to a challenge or was I really called? Unable to function, I left the ministry. One dear friend wrote to me later: "It may be a setback, but it's not a step backward or downward. It's a new way forward."

It was hard for me to see it as such. I was cognitively impaired. My mind was occupied with extreme either-or thinking. I opted for an exit plan, which was no plan at all; I just quit. Overnight I became a spiritual vagabond, wandering from one church to another, seeking something but not knowing what. That was one of the most painful transitions of my life, a disquieting period of disorientation that lasted almost four years.

Yet it was also the genesis of a deeper journey where I learned to question, evaluate, test, and adjust my perceptions and assumptions of my own identity, calling, value system, theological framework, spirituality, the church, relationships, and ultimately God's character.

My friend was right. It was a new way forward. God didn't abandon me at all. It's a lesson that is easily acknowledged but difficult to accept. In fact, my family had the opportunity to learn it some years earlier, in January 1986, when our second child was born. (We have four children).

We were very happy when she was delivered. But two hours later, the pediatrician announced that our daughter had Down syndrome. We were stunned and didn't know what to do. Friends and relatives who visited us at the hospital didn't know what to say, whether to congratulate us or to say how sorry they were. Then and there we decided to name her Joy.

A very perceptive friend wrote us a comforting note: "I wish I had wise words of comfort and counsel to share with you, but I haven't. I don't understand, and I suffer with you as you struggle for your faith in the face of what may seem to be inscrutable providence. It almost appears as a cliché to remind you that the Lord loves you, but if we lose confidence in this fundamental, eternal truth, we are lost indeed. Our heavenly Father loves you and, for some reason, has trusted you with this great disappointment and ongoing trial. He intends to demonstrate

Asia–Pacific

Pastor Song, his wife of 27 years, Nellie, and their children: (left to right) Ben, Mark, Joy, and Luke

his grace through you in a very special way. 'Thy will be done'—it's not submission merely, but acceptance."

It took me nearly four years to relearn that lesson. When I finally loosened my grip and surrendered to God in December 2005, the Lord delivered me. I experienced a marvelous touch from God and was totally healed. A week later, I met Pastor Neville Tan, who was about to undergo triple bypass surgery. He invited me to stand in as interim pastor during his medical leave. While I was willing to help, I told him bluntly that I didn't have the calling to be a pastor. I tried to distance myself from that call. After all, a need doesn't necessarily constitute a call. I'm no messiah.

But the real reason for my disclaimer was my fear. Pastor Neville understandingly nodded and said he knew God had brought me to the church. From a human perspective, my return to the ministry could be logically surmised as incidental or, at best, circumstantial. It was totally unexpected and unplanned. I got to know Pastor Neville through a chance meeting at a bowling alley.

But in God's economy, words like *incidental, circumstantial, coincidental,* and *chance* are descriptive misnomers concealing a spiritual reality waiting to be discovered and unveiled. These were actually definitive markers of my return journey to the ministry. The Lord was behind those appointments, and his call was there all along. I only saw it unraveled progressively.

The stark realities of life…

Outside the Garden of Eden

by John Ackerman
(Port-au-Prince, Haiti)

Eden. God's perfect garden and the nurse he sent me, yet anything but Haiti, the country in which I live.

It was late summer 1992 when I first met Eden in Prospere. She lived in Port-au-Prince but was visiting her father, Espasian Francois, the local Church of God pastor. That day, after I finished up at the clinic, Pastor Francois asked me to stop by, so I walked the short way to his small mud and wattle house. When I entered, he went into the bedroom and carried out a little baby girl. She was warm and cute with lots of hair, and she had just died. The baby was 14 months old, Eden's firstborn.

Since then, Eden and I have shared quite a history. Early on, she would help out at the clinic doing odd jobs. Eventually, she began nursing school, finishing her formal training as an registered nurse in about three years. Eden has worked with me ever since.

Early in 2007, she called and said she couldn't come to the clinic because she was sick. Since she was underweight and didn't eat well or exercise much, this was no surprise to me. She often had little bouts with illness, but nothing too serious. Strangely, she never bothered me with any details and just acted as if it were something normal.

A few weeks passed and Eden hadn't returned to work at the clinic. When I questioned her or Pastor Francois, they'd say she was too dizzy to stand very long but was going to a doctor and would be back as soon as she could.

As summer approached, there was still no Eden. I was confused. Everybody talked like she was fine. Even when I spoke directly to her on the phone, she gave the impression that all was well, just not well enough to return.

When I leave for home assignments, Eden runs the clinic in my absence. As that time approached in 2007, I needed to know if she

Caribbean–Atlantic

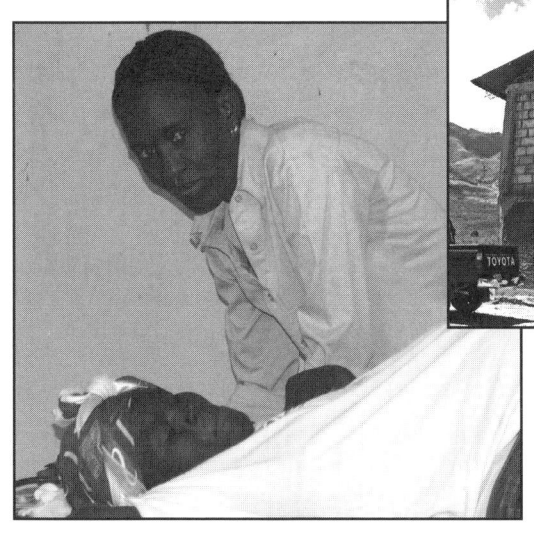

Nurse Eden conducts a prenatal examination in the clinic housed in the Prospere Church of God (above).

would be able to work. But when I pressed the family, they told me Eden was in the hospital and unable to walk due to dizziness. Finally, I decided it was time for a visit. So in late April, I picked up four family members and took an eye-opening ride.

I'd been told Eden was hospitalized on the other side of town. But her family led me to a nearby neighborhood that was very familiar to me. A few years ago, I'd spent a lot of time there with a friend. The family was surprised that I knew about San Fille Hospital. Actually, I knew more about it than they did: it is one of Mother Teresa's homes for the dying.

Initially, I couldn't bring myself to go inside, so I waited in the car. Meanwhile, Eden's family decided to take her to another hospital. When her brother carried her out in his arms, I pulled around to pick them up. As they lay Eden down on the back seat, I was shocked to see only dehydrated skin and bones. If I'd seen her in my clinic, I'd have said she was in the correct hospital.

Since the family hadn't gotten any medical records and didn't know what Eden was being treated for, I ran inside and stopped one of the Sisters of Charity to ask about the patient we were kidnapping. She was kind enough to explain in Creole that Eden had a lung infection and something in her blood. When I asked if she was saying that Eden had tuberculosis and was HIV positive, she was happy I'd understood.

Yet I Will Rejoice

After some debate with Eden's family, I took her to a lab for an HIV test. I could get results that afternoon. Then we put Eden in a hospital where she could continue on the TB medicines she'd been given at San Fille. The new hospital was also near her two children, and she'd not seen them in a long time.

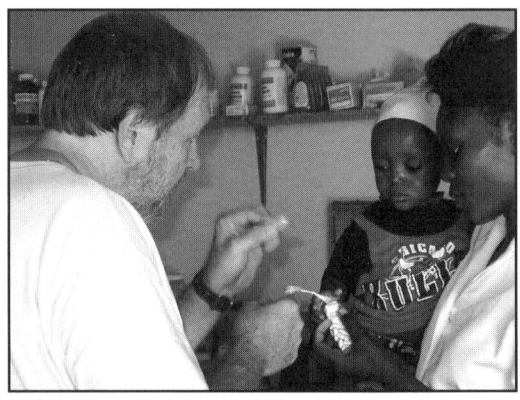

John Ackerman in his element

After the family got her settled, they left reluctantly so I could talk with her privately. Eden couldn't believe she had AIDS because she'd been faithful to her husband, but I was aware of how her husband had lived in the past. We had to know beyond a doubt.

"How will you feel if the test comes back positive?" I asked her.

Eden thought for a moment and then replied slowly, "To God be the glory. If I can do anything to bring him glory, that is what I want."

Even if she wasn't HIV positive, Eden still needed the strong TB medicines. I knew the long treatment would make her feel horrible. We hugged and I left, both of us in tears. Later that day, I was relieved to learn the tests were negative.

Eden continued the tuberculosis medicines through the summer of 2007. By October, she was back at the clinic, working with our prenatal patients again. It's as if nothing happened, but Eden's story happens again and again, and people just keep dying.

So why do we stay here in this place so far from Eden, a place where money talks, but if you don't have it—and most Haitians don't—no one listens? Even the public health department won't license the clinic because it doesn't make much money. (People come here because they can't afford to go anywhere else.) Simply put, Jodie and I believe Haiti is the place God has called us. There hasn't been a time I've thought differently. We live for the occasional minute changes we see. They keep us going and believing that God is in our work and in us as we serve here outside the garden of Eden.

An unnamed missionary praises God from within the storm.

I Am Not Alone

It's been another difficult week, and I'm wearying of it all. But last weekend, God spoke to give me strength, encouragement, and peace. Psalm 29 describes the voice of God as loud, crashing, and earth-shaking, and I suppose it is. But the overwhelming power and majesty of his voice is also realized in stillness. This is how I experienced it three times last weekend.

On Friday, I reluctantly attended a home meeting. I was just too tired—tired of holding on, of showing a calm face when inside I am in turmoil, of suppressing angry, frustrated words, of battling defensive feelings. But I'd committed to going because only there do I have a chance to know people beyond the surface. It is the only place where there is meaningful worship (for me) and where I hear deep reflections from God's Word. So, more out of sense of duty to commitment, I chose to go.

But on the way, I was steeling myself. That takes enormous energy, because you must be vulnerable and let down your guard in order to worship genuinely. As we began, my translator whispered that she wouldn't be able to help me on a project after all. That was the last straw; I had nothing left with which to hold on. It was a little predicament in the larger scheme of challenges, but I didn't have the reserve to solve one more problem, even a little one. Yet I couldn't leave without sending the wrong message, so I battled on tearfully. I could barely control my emotions, and it was very clear to everyone that something was wrong.

Finally, the end was in sight. But then the question came: Who would like prayer? I knew I couldn't speak, so I simply raised my hand, and several came to be with me. The group leader began praying but then stopped. I thought she was waiting on God until suddenly I realized that someone was at my feet. Opening my eyes, I saw the leader and her mother kneeling on the floor with a tub of sudsy water.

"May we wash your feet?" they asked me.

Sensing their loving concern, I broke down completely and couldn't stop sobbing. They washed and dried my feet, hugged me, and prayed.

Yet I Will Rejoice

In that moment, I heard God's voice of understanding, strength, and peace coming to me quietly through his people.

On Saturday, I went to the office to check e-mails, which would be a miracle to get as the server and Internet are sporadic. Surprisingly, everything was working and I found an e-mail from a friend. She too had attended a home meeting. There a member shared that she had awakened that morning knowing that she must pray urgently for me. She did, and the entire group also prayed for me that evening. Once again, I heard the voice of God. It was the voice of comfort to me through God's people.

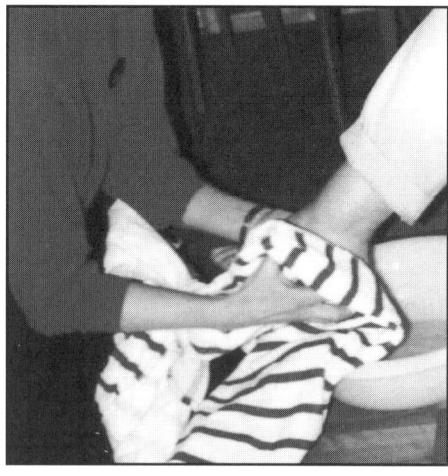
"May we wash your feet?" they asked me.

On Sunday, I joined over 300 people at the fourth anniversary celebration of a certain church. Two women on the program were to give testimonies. I recognized them from worshiping there before and also because I'd spoken at their retreat a year earlier. One of them approached me and said, "You prayed for me at the retreat—that God would change my character. I am here to testify that God has indeed changed it!" It wasn't my prayer alone, of course, but her words were the voice of encouragement to me through God's people.

I went into my office on Monday. Nothing had changed; the problems with solutions yet to be found were still there; I still struggled to know when and what to speak. Although I was the only person there, I knew I was not alone. Steeling myself against the harsh realities of the storm here can protect me somewhat, but that kind of steel blocks God's transforming grace in my life. I wonder how much of his grace I have missed while trying to be strong in myself.

I praise God for reminding me in so many ways that I am not alone. Though challenges sometimes overwhelm me, I want to respond as the prophet who vowed, "Yet I will rejoice in the Lord, I will be joyful in God my Savior" (Habakkuk 3:18).

Thirty-five years of ministry in the Caribbean–Atlantic began…

UNDER A MANGO TREE

by Kelvin Harrinarine
(Carapichaima, Trinidad)

"A farmer went out to sow his seed. As he was scattering the seed, some fell along the path…Some fell on rock…Other seed fell among thorns… Still other seed fell on good soil. It came up and yielded a crop, a hundred times more than was sown" (Luke 8:5–8).

My name is Kelvin Dominic Harrinarine. Although my wife Minnie is Guyanese and I am Trinidadian, we have many things in common. We are both of East Indian descent, we are the parents of four children, and we both have salvation stories in which American missionaries played a role. Minnie was saved under the ministry of Ralph Coolidge, a missionary in Guyana in the 1960s. As for myself, here is my story.

I am 58 years old now. But as a little boy of about seven or eight years, I attended Sunday school under a mango tree next to where I lived in La Pastora. It was conducted by students of West Indies Bible Institute (now West Indies Theological College).

In 1959, I was invited with all the Sunday school children to the opening of a new Church of God, Houston Memorial, on the Bible school campus. I remember that Sunday morning very vividly for two reasons: I arrived late, and it was the first time I had ever entered a church building in my life.

After the dedication service, I observed that all the children had a Sunday school leaflet in their possession, but I had none. So I approached a white lady and asked for one. To my surprise, she turned to her little daughter, standing next to her, and requested that she give hers to me. Later, I learned that the woman's name was Betty Jo Johnson. She was a missionary in Trinidad. Her daughter's name was Don Deena. Today Don Deena is a missionary in Lebanon.

I continued attending Church of God services in that new chapel, as well as Sunday school. As I got older, I joined the youth fellowship and

Kelvin Harrinarine and the chapel where he first went to church

also accepted Christ. I was baptized at Carlos Street Church of God by another missionary, Jack C. Ryan, in 1965.

Called into the ministry, I enrolled at West Indies Bible Institute in 1968—the very school whose students had first introduced me to Jesus under a mango tree. I was the first local person to attend the Bible school, graduating in 1972. Later, I returned to campus to pastor that congregation.

The story seems to have come full circle. My last son, Selvin, graduated from West Indies Theological College in 2007 with a bachelor of arts degree in psychology and counseling.

In addition to pastoring five different congregations, I have served the church in many other ways. Currently, I am executive secretary of the General Assembly of the Church of God in Trinidad and Tobago and also chair the executive committee of the college. After 35 years in the ministry, it remains my desire today to serve Jesus however he leads.

I am eternally grateful for the students of West Indies Bible Institute who planted seeds under a mango tree more than 45 years ago. I believe it was good soil there, and the harvest continues.

CARIBBEAN–ATLANTIC

Grappling with God about life's hard questions…

THINGS YOU THINK BUT NEVER SAY

by Phil Murphy
(Lake Wales, Florida)

I was in a hotel room in Santo Domingo, Dominican Republic, when the call came at 3:00 in the morning. My friend Tim was on the other end. His first words were, "Phil, I have bad news." I braced myself for the worst. He went on to tell me how 15 armed men had broken into the home of Tania and Franky Desir, our orphanage director, and kidnapped their three-year-old daughter.

After hearing of the violent attack, I dropped to my knees and cried out to God. I quickly felt a peace as far as God was concerned. After claiming to follow Christ since I was nine years old, I've been around the block several times regarding my personal beliefs about God. It all climaxed a few years ago in Haiti. Like most people, I'd struggled for many years with the age-old questions of why bad things happen to good people, how God can allow evil, and why bad happens even when you are doing good for others. Since coming to Haiti in 1986, Lonnie and I both had contracted malaria more than 24 times and typhoid twice. My son, daughter, and I all had hepatitis A, and David almost died from an allergic reaction to medicines. Lonnie had been robbed once at gunpoint, our house had been broken into, and a bad land deal cost the orphanage over $40,000. I'd watched Haiti slowly slide into functioning chaos, seen dozens of dead bodies, some of them murdered and then burned, and seen children suffering from malnutrition. How could I not question God?

After God and I struggled long and honestly, we'd come to an agreement: I no longer held God responsible for things that happen in this life. I came to the only conclusion I could: It may be unpopular and disturbing to many folks, but I've decided that God is somehow limited. I most definitely cannot hold him accountable for the evil that humans do, and I cannot expect him to be Superman to fly into every situation and

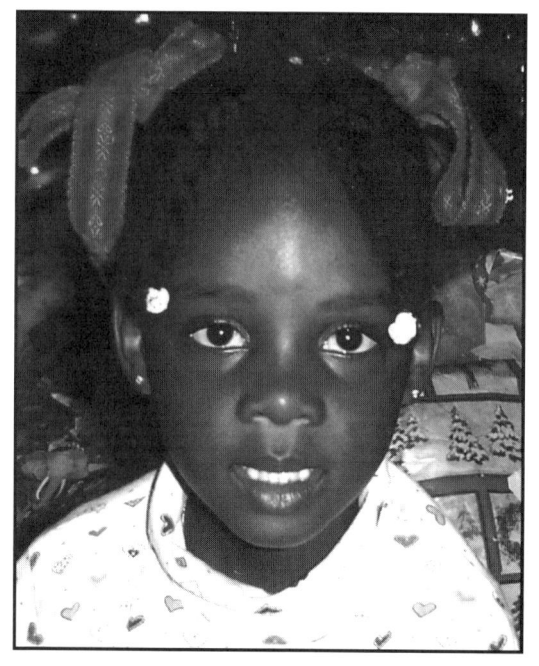

Three-year-old Fabbie Desir

save people. But no matter what I've been through or the evil I've observed, I've also seen a very steady, quiet force at work. I call it grace—the healing and reconciling power of God. I've seen Romans 8:28 ring true over and over again: "In all things God works for the good of those who love him, who have been called according to his purpose."

All of this is to say that through the kidnapping of Fabbie, who in all practical senses is our granddaughter, I never once blamed God or was angry with him. But I found myself angry just the same. My faith in humans was at an all-time low. Since my life has been dedicated to helping people, I was confused. I couldn't seem to pick up the pieces or even find the desire to look for the pieces I needed to pick up.

Instead, I found myself sometimes breaking into sweat as rage welled up inside for no apparent reason. I realized I'd lost my compassion for the Haitian people and that my patience with them was all but gone. As I woke up every morning, I determined to have a better day, yet at some point, some tiny thing would set me off. Luckily, I never really lost my temper, but the rage seemed to be right under the surface. I was angry that Haitians don't look at the world the way I do and that I seemed to care more about them and their country than they do. I was infuriated that Haiti seems to be moving backwards instead of forwards, no matter how much time, energy, and money is poured into it. I was furious that Haitians have been so beaten down for 200 years that they refuse to stand up for themselves or one another. I was livid that the community did not storm the house that night Franky and Tania's little girl was taken to protect them and destroy those who sought to destroy and steal life. I was angry at myself that I was several hours away and couldn't fix the problem. And once I returned, I was angry that I couldn't produce answers or bring Fabbie back home.

Still, I could see grace, healing, and reconciliation taking place. During this time, several people we'd been estranged from were comforting and helpful. The day before the kidnappers released Fabbie, I stopped by the house to see the family. When I walked in, there sat three girls who'd been raised in our home with Tania, two of whom had left us on bad terms and angry at Tania. I was touched because I knew the history between all of us and because they lived far away. They had made a huge effort to come. A few minutes later, a fourth girl arrived, and I was blessed again. All four decided to ride to our house and see Lonnie. When she walked out of her office and saw them, her knees went weak and she burst into tears of pain and joy. They all wept and hugged for several minutes.

For those reading my raw thoughts and emotions and trying to find a theological slant, don't. I'm not saying that God allowed or caused the kidnapping; I no longer can believe that way. What I am saying is, despite all that is evil, God never tires from doing good. If the Devil roams the earth like a lion seeking all he may devour, then God is a restless wind always moving and seeking a crack to enter some place to fill with grace, healing, and reconciliation.

> *No matter what is meant for evil, God is ever present and seeking an entry to do good.*

I am still angry, still in that dark and lonely place, a valley of indecision and shadow. I'm not sure I can trust myself to do what I've done many times before—reach deep down and find my source of strength and courage to move forward. I doubt if I can ever feel the way I did prior to the kidnapping or that I have what it takes to move beyond this point in my life. But I am sure that I can trust God to do what God does. I am confident that no matter what is meant for evil, God is ever present and seeking an entry to do good in the hearts and lives of people. Perhaps this seems to some like a very weak God, but not to me. I say it is a very determined and strong God who can stand up to the wicked and evil things of this life and not quit. I say it is a God of unquenchable love

Phil Murphy, Tania Desir, and her children

and mercy who can continue on in the face of injustice, torture, hatred, and greed.

Most importantly, I am glad that God is God—the way he is and the way he functions. That kind of love, desire, and commitment inspires me in my darkness like a tiny spark in a wet and gloomy place. I find hope in the fact that even if I do not have the strength and courage to go on, that restless wind is blowing all around and over me, seeking an entry to fill me with grace, healing, and reconciliation.

After five days of intense trauma and negotiations, a ransom was paid and Fabbie Desir was returned to her family. Through his faithful love and grace, God used friends, family, and patience to bring me out of that pit of darkness. Once more, I am in a place where I can live, love, and trust again.

All he wanted was a pair of socks.

A Christmas Perspective

by David and Kathy Simpson
(Plovdiv, Bulgaria)

At the beginning of December, the church leaders in Plovdiv decided to do something to help the needy at Christmastime. We have been in the apartments of many of the 30 or so folks in our little fellowship. We know they usually heat only one room in the winter, wash dishes in cold water to save a few pennies, and consider more than two or three outfits of clothing a luxury. In the United States, we might call these folks the poorest of the poor. But like their ancient Macedonian neighbors, out of their extreme poverty welled up rich generosity.[*]

The group chose to provide gifts for the 45 children in the Panagyurishte Orphanage. Bulgaria has many homes for youngsters ages 6 through 18. Some of the residents were abandoned by their parents. Many others were voluntarily surrendered because their families could not afford to support them. These children often spend holidays with parents or grandparents. We learned that the Panagyurishte home serves youth without mothers or fathers. They are utterly alone and with the barest of resources.

The items assembled for the children would not be on the request list of any American child, but we knew they represented sacrificial giving for the Bulgarians. The church ladies prepared 45 bags, each with a toothbrush, toothpaste, soap, tissue packet, chocolate bar, hard candies, tangerine, and a Christian storybook. In addition, people had collected piles of used clothing and shoes. As we drove to the orphanage, we cringed at the thought of giving gifts that would be shunned by children from our Indiana hometown.

We steeled ourselves before entering the building. We knew it would be drab and dirty, but we were surprised at the temperature. The chil-

---

[*] 2 Corinthians 8:2 paraphrased

Yet I Will Rejoice

Bulgarian orphan children overjoyed with secondhand clothes

dren and staff were all wearing their coats inside. The small space heater warmed only a fraction of the activity room. It certainly wasn't cozy and welcoming, but the kids greeted us with enthusiasm. They gathered around for hugs and to see what we had brought. We quickly passed out the bags. In no time, they were eating the tangerines, comparing the colors of the toothbrushes, and thanking us over and over. Several children showed their appreciation by offering us a piece of their candy. We were overwhelmed that these destitute little ones wanted to give something to us.

Next was the distribution of the secondhand clothes. The kids sorted through the piles and helped each other find things that fit. They eagerly took the items that we had been nervous about bringing. There were smiles on so many faces, but not all. One boy was distressed. "Are there any more socks? I just wanted a pair of socks," he wept. All the socks were gone and he wasn't consoled by a sweater or a pair of pants. We had to depart without fulfilling his simple wish for socks.

Europe–Middle East

Before the Christmas Eve service, we reported the events of the day to Nenka. She had been ill and unable to go with us. As the church leader, she thanked the group for their contributions and Christian service. However, she too was haunted by the image of the little fellow wanting socks. She was also horrified to learn that although each child had a blanket, their beds didn't have sheets. She urged everyone to go to the bazaar that week and purchase socks and sheets. Nenka asked them to ensure that each child would receive a new pair of socks and a bottom sheet.

"God has blessed us with more than we need," she challenged the group, although each person knew poverty firsthand. "We can bless these children in the name of Christ."

As the apostle Paul commended the charity of the Macedonians to the Corinthians, we commend the generosity of these Bulgarian Christians to you. We pray that we all will be inspired by their example of sacrificial giving. We also thank God who blessed us with the greatest gift of all, his Son, Jesus Christ.

Attacked!
by Carol VanHayden (Moscow, Russia)

Before school began, I attended a staff retreat outside Moscow. One morning, I went out to walk and have devotions. I found out two things quickly: you must always know the territory well, and Russian guard dogs have long chains. In a moment, a Rotweiler mix attacked me while still chained and managed to bite me four times. Two ladies witnessed the dog attack and immediately laid hands on me, praying for me in Russian. At our conference, I was prayed for again. That evening the S.O.S. clinic recommended the rabies vaccination, which I took.

It is easy to get busy and into the territory of spiritual neglect. When we do, we are risking unknown territory where anything can happen. Sometimes, it isn't until we get to the end of our rope (or chain) and get a few bites that we realize we need to get back to the safety of the Lord. I thank God for being with me and rescuing me!

A horrible automobile accident taught me I was…

In the Shepherd's Arms

by Klara Rauleder
(Haiterbach, Germany)

It was Sunday, July 19, 1992. We had guests, so I got up earlier than usual and started cooking dinner before we drove to church in two cars. Afterwards, I wanted to leave right away so I could finish cooking, but Waldemar, my husband, was eager to show our guests the Black Forest before we returned.

I can't recall the day clearly, but it was hot. I also remember the children's excitement and my annoyance at their jockeying for positions in the cars. Finally, I announced, "Enough! Just get in! We're leaving!" Everyone piled in, but I can't remember who rode where. As we drove, I began to feel sick from the heat and thought maybe we should rest along the way. But dinner preparations were waiting, and I knew we'd be home soon.

The next thing I remember is waking up in a hospital. Three weeks had passed. I was wearing a neck stabilizer and had a cast on my right arm. "Where am I? What day is it?" I asked, wondering if I'd missed my son's birthday.

"Klara, you're in the hospital," my mother answered. "You had an accident."

I asked about my children and learned they were all right. I wanted to see them but was told I needed to rest. My mother wouldn't say more because the doctor had said not to tell me everything. A few days later, the doctor gave in to my demands for answers, and I learned the truth. Julia, the eldest daughter, had a broken collarbone; my son Arnold had facial wounds; Ronald, my nephew, had a broken leg; and our daughter Ines had a broken arm. Then I heard the worst: our six-year-old daughter was dead. My world collapsed with this news. Margarethe was to turn seven in September. Now she would never see that birthday or any other.

Try as I might, I couldn't remember the accident. Julia, who'd sat up front with me, explained that I'd suddenly passed out. When my head hit the steering wheel, our car veered into the other lane and collided head on with another car. Margarethe and the other driver had been killed.

When I was finally released from the hospital, I asked the medical staff to document my injuries. They answered that a full sheet of paper wasn't space enough to list everything. Among the injuries were a cracked skull, a severed neck vertebra, and a broken arm, pelvis, and ribs.

On top of these, the crack in my cranium had taken its toll on my vision. At first, the world looked upside down. Then everything disappeared from my sight. For a while, the pain was so great I couldn't cry. I felt like I was living in a thick fog. Deep within me, I sensed an empty hole that was impossible to fill. Even though a Bible lay before me on a table, I had no inclination even to pick it up, much less read it. Thoughts spun wildly in my head. Was there any point in my living? Does God even exist? If he does, why did he let this horrible accident happen?

Klara and Waldemar Rauleder and two of their children, Ines and Matthias, who was born after the accident

Yet I Will Rejoice

The Church of God in Haiterbach, Germany, where Klara and her family are active members

Later, I realized how important it was that my husband stood by me through this painful and difficult time of questioning. The understanding and help from brothers and sisters in the church and others were invaluable. We were supported by caring hands. It was as a healing salve to hear that many people were praying for us, even people in other countries. A married couple came each night to study the Bible and pray with me.

In the worst of this dark time, our pastor encouraged me by relating how shepherds care for their flocks. When a herd must cross a river, the shepherd takes a lamb in his arms and carries it to the other side. The lamb's mother follows her child, bringing the entire herd along. So it was in my case. I'd been carried in the Shepherd's arms and the whole church had followed along. This picture renewed my courage and continues to help me even today.

God healed me emotionally and spiritually, but also physically. Miraculously, I gave birth to my fifth child on February 11, 1994, less than two years after the accident. Waldemar and I named him Matthias, which means "gift of God."

Today, another of God's gifts is that I am a grandmother. With God's help, I am functioning well each day, but I also look forward to seeing Margarethe again. I pray with all my heart that many others will come with us to the heavenly paradise waiting at the end of our journey.

EUROPE–MIDDLE EAST

Could I possibly find her among thousands?

MIRACLE IN FLORENCE

by Susan English
(Central Asia)

I am a teacher, but not in Italy or anywhere else in Europe. But when my good friends announced they were traveling there, I decided to join them. Little did I know the adventure I was about to have. And to think that I almost cancelled when my friends did.

About eight years ago, a very good Asian friend moved to Italy. An artist, she had been a university art teacher, but she wanted to study more. Michelangelo and the Italian Renaissance had made Florence famous, so that's where my friend moved. Although she called me a few times, we eventually lost contact. I had no e-mail address, no phone number, no apartment address, and no way to contact her. But now I was headed to Italy myself. Before I left home, I asked friends to pray that somehow I would find Flora. Never mind that Florence is a city of 350,000. Couldn't God perform a miracle?

On our first day there, another friend and I both kept looking for Flora wherever we went. We purposefully visited an area famous for its street artists thinking she might be there, but we didn't find her. Still I wasn't worried. I just kept telling God that if I was to find Flora, he would have to make it happen.

After my friend left Florence the next morning, I started touring museums. As I was exiting my second museum around noon, I spotted Flora! Since Florence is home to the most Renaissance art and architecture in the world, there are not just a few museums in the city. Yet there she was, near the very museum I had chosen to visit, and just at the time I was leaving. She was walking my way on an obscure street with few people. I just stood there waiting for her to come close enough to see me, all the while smiling in amazement.

Finally, Flora looked up and noticed me. But, she told me later, she thought it was someone who only looked like me. After all, why would

Yet I Will Rejoice

Flora enjoying the beautiful architecture of Florence, Italy

I be in Florence, Italy? But when she got about ten feet away, she knew it was me. It will be one of those moments in life I will never forget. We hugged and kissed on each cheek, Italian style, and I announced that God had helped me find her.

Adding to the amazement of it all, Flora told me that this was not an area of town she usually visited. But she had some court business there that day. Under normal circumstances, she shouldn't have been there. Of course, under normal circumstances, I wouldn't have been there either. Only God could have orchestrated our meeting.

We spent the next two days together. I had my own personal tour guide, translator, and art expert. Flora speaks fluent Italian, which confused people greatly. They couldn't wrap their brains around the fact that she spoke Italian, I didn't speak Italian, and the two of us communicated in yet another language. We enjoyed how we baffled people.

Finally, I realized why I had to go to Italy. If it had been up to me, I would have dropped out as soon as my friends did. In fact, I tried to cancel but couldn't. I truly believe God wanted me to spend time with Flora. It was a miracle that I found her and an amazing two days of my life. At this point, only God understands this miracle completely, and that's okay with me. I'm happy just to have been part of it all.

Europe–Middle East

She went to sleep and met God face to face.

Sweet Grandma Mary

by Lena Barannikova
(Chelyabinsk, Russia)

She came from the Ukraine, the perfect fairy-tale grandma—very pleasant-looking, smiling, and shy. We called her Grandma Mary. But her living conditions were far from fairy-tale perfect. She shared just one single room and a small kitchen with a daughter and two grandsons.

After her accident, we visited her and were amazed at her tiny apartment. But we soon forgot the surroundings as we talked with Grandma Mary and realized her bright sense of humor. She was so happy we'd come, she wouldn't let us go until we ate lunch and drank tea together. Her only complaint was that she couldn't move freely because of her broken leg. She'd always wanted to help her daughters, but now she needed to be helped herself.

But Grandma Mary had no self pity, even though life was difficult. She'd come to the Urals long before. When she learned that her daughter Galina, a single mother of two small boys, was having trouble making ends meet, Mary's only desire was to rush to her side to help her. Her house was sold for almost nothing—barely enough to cover the train ticket to Chelyabinsk—but the chance to help her family was worth all she had.

Once she arrived in Chelyabinsk, she wanted to find a new church home. Mary liked the feel of the worship in a certain place, but leaders there questioned her about her previous church, its registration, and more. Finally, they agreed to allow her to attend their services but not to participate in Communion. Disappointed, Mary decided to continue searching for a new church family, bringing her to the big hall rented by our church. Instinctively, Mary knew that she had found her new family. From then on, Grandma Mary could always be found sitting close to the preacher and listening carefully to everything he had to say. At last, she was completely happy.

Yet I Will Rejoice

Sweet Grandma Mary and the Church of God worshiping in Chelyabinsk

Soon she began supporting the church however she could. If a project needed money, she was always among the first to participate. She never missed a single women's conference and was always there with a Bible and notebook. Because she spoke Ukranian, it wasn't always easy to understand her words, but no one could miss her bright and thankful spirit. When she prayed, her heart burned with love for the Lord and with thankfulness for her family, food, home, and the Bible.

This passionate spirit came through as we prayed together a few Sundays ago. Then last Sunday, she missed church. We knew she was sick, although she joked whenever her stomach hurt that she should follow a healthier diet. We prayed that the Lord would heal her and that she could participate in our next women's conference. But Grandma Mary passed away last Thursday. We hadn't known that she had cancer. She prayed that God would take her home without long suffering and that she wouldn't burden her family, and the Lord answered her request. She went to sleep one night and, without waking, met God face to face in the morning.

We're happy for her, of course, but it's hard to believe that her place in the church is now empty. Still, it's impossible not to smile whenever I think about her because her own smiling face is etched in my mind. I can even hear her laughter. Sweet Grandma Mary was always an angel to her daughters' families and our church. She was an angel who touched me too.

Europe–Middle East

Despite difficult circumstances, they hope.

I Will Stand and Watch

by Don Deena Johnson
(Beirut, Lebanon)

Situated next door to an auto repair shop in a shopping district just north of Beirut, the apartment is off a back alley and up a couple flights of stairs. I walked through the main door and encountered a long hallway, its walls covered with announcements and displays of groups of Philippine women studying the Bible and worshiping together. It was a Sunday morning and the vibrant beat of tambourine, drums, and guitar drew me to the open door at the end of the hallway. The joyous singing compelled me to enter and join in with the group of women (and a few men), 50 strong and growing, who gather here every Sunday.

Foreign workers constitute a massive presence in Lebanon. Thirty percent of the official work force of one and a half million people is foreign and serves primarily in homes as domestic workers or outdoors in construction. They typically work 12- to 15-hour days for very low wages in order to support family members back home. Abuse is not uncommon. Denied the right even to hold their own passport if employed through an agency, these men and women have little recourse when a situation becomes intolerable. Nevertheless, this Philippine congregation, meeting together under the legal coverage of the Church of God in Lebanon, shares the hope and grace of Jesus Christ every Sunday and is intent upon evangelizing and discipling Lebanon's Filipinos.

Pastora Jemima Escala leads this growing community, which recently planted a new congregation in another section of Beirut. She is herself a domestic worker who felt called by God to return to Lebanon to encourage and minister to her own people. The team of leaders working with her makes full use of Sundays, the only day off the women have. Bible study is followed by morning worship. After eating lunch together, the women gather for discipleship training or go out in small groups to witness to other Filipinos taking advantage of their own day off. The day concludes with music practice to prepare for the next Sunday's worship. For those who may have an evening off, there are Bible studies in nine different locations around the city during the week. Pastora, as this community affectionately calls her, cleans houses to live but lives to nurture the spiritual journey of Filipinos so far away from their homes.

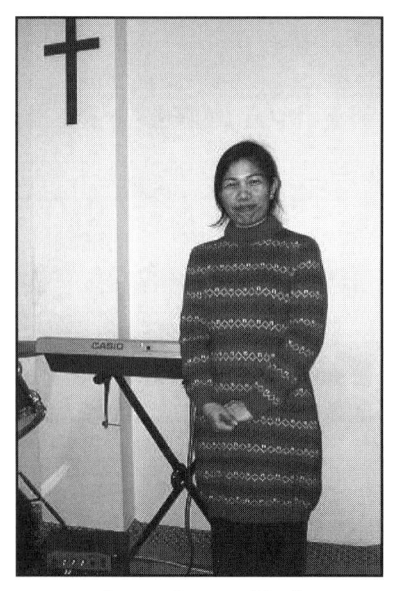

Pastora Jemima Escala

We had finished singing. The tambourines with their colorful streamers were put under the chairs. The air was warm and damp as we waited for a young man to approach the front. Ernesto began his testimony with a shy smile:

> Two years ago, my wife Mareline and I were in the Philippines. We had applied with an agency to work overseas. She was going to Hong Kong and I was going to Dubai. We didn't want to live apart, but you can't find places for couples very often, so we prayed that if it was God's will we could find somewhere for both of us. One day, I read of a family in Lebanon that wanted a couple. It was going to be difficult because we already were promised to Hong Kong and Dubai. But, praise God, we were able to come.
>
> We're glad to be here together, but this has been very difficult. Our employer is hard, and we're treated very badly sometimes. For a whole year, we didn't get one day off. At night when we prayed together, we cried to God for a church. We wanted some place where we could serve the Lord and worship, but we didn't even get a day off.
>
> Finally, I heard God say, "Why don't you ask? Tell your employer why you want time off." I was afraid, but eventually I asked. He

Europe–Middle East

Leading worship with tambourines; Ernesto and Mareline singing their testimony (inset)

agreed we could have the last Sunday off every month. I pray to be here every Sunday, but thank God he has answered this far. I will stand and watch to see how God will continue to answer. He is faithful. Praise God.

This small congregation has very little of the world's material possessions, but they have accomplished much by God's Spirit working among them. They take seriously God's Word, which says to rejoice in all circumstances. Yet even in their rejoicing, they haven't stopped dreaming. They expect that one day soon, in Junieh, a city in which a Bible study group is meeting, a new congregation will be planted for the glory of God.

Yet I Will Rejoice

Violence continues, but the children feel…

The Strong Arms of Christ

by Paul and Brenda Maxfield
(Anderson, Indiana)

The airplane hit a pocket of air and lurched violently, causing the cups of juice to tumble off our tray tables onto the floor. The man across the aisle began fanning himself nervously. We looked at each other in alarm. We were already on alert taking this trip in the first place. Stories of assassination and kidnapping were rampant in the area of Colombia where we were going. Being gringos, we knew we were in more danger. Even though we speak fluent Spanish, our faces would give us away.

The ride became smoother. We looked out the window and saw the propellers whirling contentedly and felt reassured. The jungle stretched out below in verdant greens. There was not a home in sight, only masses of lush trees and bush surrounded by sprawling mountains. It was hard to believe that groups of paramilitary forces and the opposing guerrillas roamed those mountains, eager to shoot each other or anyone else who got in their way. We were entering the heart of Colombia's largest coca-growing region (the raw plant material used to make cocaine).

Children of Promise, whom we represented, began helping children in this area in 1999. Since then, sponsored children have received food, school fees and supplies, and medical care, relieving the desperation of church families and supporting those who have taken in orphans.

We landed with no problems and made our way to the church where the children and their families awaited us. We settled onto wobbly plastic chairs and were treated to a wonderful program. The children sang, recited scripture, and gave choral readings. We watched their love of the Lord joyfully. They had suffered greatly, yet were now smiling and performing with abandon. Later, as we interviewed each child and their family members, we began to see the true picture of their suffering.

Latin America

Paul and Brenda Maxfield with sponsored children from Colombia

There was little Marco*, eight years old. His dad was murdered by guerrillas and thrown into the river, where family found his body floating. Eight months later, in a different village, his mother was killed. Shortly after that, his maternal grandparents were killed. Marco lives with his remaining grandma. Despite the fear and insecurity that have marked his life, Marco sat before us, smiling shyly and telling us to thank his sponsor and that he likes to eat rice.

For the last six years, Maria, age 13, has lived with her grandmother across the border in Ecuador. They have an outhouse, candles for light, and the river for water. Every day, Maria takes a boat across the river to attend school in Colombia. They live so remotely they can only attend church every two or three weeks when a church elder ventures through the jungle to their home to hold services.

Before moving there, Maria lived with her parents in town. Her father was shot and killed by the paramilitary. One year later, Maria was

---

* All names have been changed.

walking across the street holding her mother's hand. Suddenly, the sound of a bullet exploded and her mother slumped to the pavement, her hand slipping from Maria's grasp. Maria looked in horror at her dead mother and went running, screaming to neighbors for help.

Maria and her mother had simply been in the wrong place at the wrong time. A common tactic of both guerrillas and paramilitary is control by fear. What better way to instill fear than to arbitrarily shoot people? Even after six years, one can still feel Maria's fear. As Paul was taking pictures of her, she started to fidget. "Who are you really?" she asked, meaning, "Can I trust you?" Paul reassured Maria, and she sighed with relief. When we then asked her who her best friend was, she looked directly at us and answered simply, "Dios," meaning God.

> *Masked men with automatic weapons had opened fire. The eyes of the children we'd met flashed before us. What if it had been them?*

Next we met Sophia, who is eight. Her father was dragged from their home, suspected of cooperating with the paramilitary. There were no questions asked and no trial before he was shot and left for dead. But he wasn't dead, so he began to crawl away to save himself and his family. He crawled for three kilometers, leaving a trail of blood. The guerrillas realized their mistake, followed the blood, and shot him again, this time dead.

Sophia's mother remarried and left her to go to another village 12 hours away. During childbirth, she became paralyzed from the waist down. Now Sophia never sees her and has been adopted by her grandparents. They brag as they talk of Sophia. "She's really smart. She loves animals. If she ever gets a few pesos, she'll buy a chicken. Then we have eggs." Sophia tells us that she likes math.

Latin America

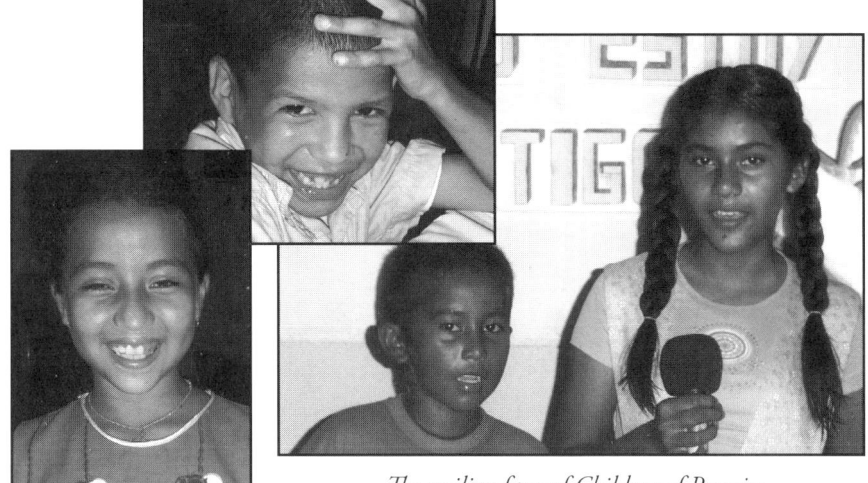

The smiling faces of Children of Promise

We hadn't been back home two days when we were horrified to read that masked men with automatic weapons had opened fire in the Christian and Missionary Alliance Church just blocks from the Church of God where we'd been. At least three people were killed. Fourteen were wounded, some of them children. The eyes of the children we'd met flashed before us. What if it had been them?

So the violence continues. But what also continues is the presence of Christ in a very unique way. Unmet sponsors from across the ocean and local Colombian Christians work hand in hand to offer comfort, hope, and long-term care for those terrorized and haunted by conflict. Where would these children be if it were not for people who cared beyond their own families, beyond their own comfort zones, beyond their own agendas?

Through this partnership, Marco, Maria, Sophia, and 41 other children in Puerto Asis feel the strong arms of Christ around them in the hugs they receive at church and in the necessities of daily life provided for them by sponsors. They also know the love and compassion of Christ in the church people who have become their families. Christ is there. They can go on. And they will never forget.

This story is condensed from an article published in the June/July 2005 issue of ONEvoice! *magazine, copyright © 2005 by Church of God Ministries, Inc. Used by permission.*

From Germany, to America, to Argentina…

South America on My Heart

by Manuel Killisch
(Leandro N. Alem, Misiones, Argentina)

What are you doing here?" I asked Franco Santonocito, longtime missionary to Egypt, when I saw him in a friend's car pulling out of the parking lot of Church of God Ministries.

"I'm looking for you," he answered, obviously trying to recruit a young seminary student for the mission field.

"Nice try," I thought and returned to my reflection paper for Old Testament that was due the next morning.

I was studying in my second year at Anderson University School of Theology. Coming to Anderson from Germany had been the greatest challenge of my life. I left behind a promising career as a concert violist in Europe and definitely wasn't ready for the next adventure—not yet.

One year later, as my studies were coming to an end, I found myself deeply depressed. Without a place to serve and no idea about what to do next, I questioned the decisions I had made as I struggled through the semester. The comment of a friend in Germany before I left for the United States resounded in my ear: "No one said it would be easy."

Change came one Tuesday morning during chapel. A professor was about to give his farewell speech to the seminary community. Sitting in the last pew, carrying out my responsibilities as the chapel assistant, I was more or less attentive to the service until the professor went forward to take his seat on a chair placed in front of the beautiful stained glass window. That window had often made me pause to meditate on its meaning. At that very moment, God pulled me out of my depression with a deep sense of assurance that all the semesters of preparation had served a purpose. I knew there was a place for me to serve. I had never experienced such an instantaneous certainty before. It was shaking, and I knew it came from the Lord.

I made an appointment with my mentor and dear friend, Dr. J. (Students called Juanita Leonard by this name to express our respect and love

Manuel Killisch preaching (left) and playing with Argentinean children

for this woman of faith.) She opened her office door smiling and asked me to share my experience. After I had finished my story, she looked at me and said simply, "I know." For the second time in days, I was shaken by the Lord. How did she know? Dr. J. told me that for a long time she had been praying that God would show me his goal for my life.

I began asking God for his guidance and he blessed me with the advice of wise brothers and sisters. My pastor told me, "Manuel, you are like Paul. You are a Hebrew. You are a Roman citizen, and you're doing quite well in Antioch." He was right. I've never had problems adjusting to different cultures and places. More and more, God put South America on my heart. I began praying in this direction.

One morning, I went to see my friend Randy Bargerstock. He had served for many years as a missionary in Argentina. I asked him if he knew about a possibility to serve there in a teaching and leadership development role. Randy looked at me for a while without saying anything. Then he answered, "Argentina just called and asked me this very question." Even cold Germans have emotions, and I could feel the tears filling my eyes. Now I was ready for the next adventure.

> *Even cold Germans have emotions, and I could feel the tears filling my eyes.*

Shortly after this, I received an invitation from the Church of God in Argentina. Almost 50 years ago, my grandparents went to Argentina as missionaries from Germany. Could it be that God continues his call within a family?

My last semester in seminary was spent finding ways to get onto the mission field. In March 2007, Global Missions of Church of God Ministries and the national churches in Germany and Argentina began an exciting partnership to equip leaders and pastors for the ministry in Argentina. I am blessed to be part of this wonderful journey. Every time I leave a local congregation after having taught a seminar, I can feel how God has changed my life. Did my seminary education equip me for every situation I would face? No. But it opened my eyes and heart for the people of Argentina. They need to hear a word from the Lord, and so do we. Are we ready for the great adventure?

Manuel with students at a youth convention

LATIN AMERICA

Except for a miracle, the outcome was certain.

THE BATTLE THAT PRAYER WON

by Luz Gonzales
(Duncanville, Texas)

You must sign this document to be on the government's safe list!"

This stern message was delivered to Carlos Lamelas by the secret police when they unexpectedly showed up late one night at his home in Atanagildo, Cuba.

I met Carlos in 1996 at the Inter-American Conference meeting in Cuba. Since it was my first time in that country, I was eager to learn everything I could, so I approached a young pastor and introduced myself.

Happily, Pastor Carlos invited me to visit his church. As I got to know him, I was impressed by his passion, vision, and desire to evangelize. His wife Uramis prepared a tasty meal, which surprised me since food is limited in Cuba. (She ignored my question about how she'd managed such a meal with the severe food rationing. Later, I learned that when visitors are coming, Cubans save up whatever food they can, sometimes for months. I pondered their sacrifice and how they survived on their meager earnings: eight to ten dollars a month for a pastor, ten dollars for a teacher, and only twenty for a doctor.)

As we visited, I recognized Carlos' potential and leadership qualities. When he asked me to be his mentor, I readily accepted and soon was busy answering his many questions. Each time I went to Cuba, I took books, cassettes, CDs, and other materials for him and other pastors. Carlos studied everything diligently and distinguished himself as a pastor who truly loves both God and the Church of God.

It wasn't until my third trip to Cuba that Carlos shared about the unexpected visit from the secret police. When they pressured him for his signature, he replied, "I won't sign. I will not commit to any earthly government because I am already committed to Jesus Christ." Although they threatened him, he steadfastly refused. Perhaps out of fear, many pastors from various churches did sign; however, others declined. Shortly thereafter, the harassment and persecution of pastors began.

Carlos was elected president of the Church of God in Cuba in November 2002. Subsequently, he resigned his church and moved to Havana, the church's headquarters. One day, without warning or explanation, the secret police knocked on his door and escorted him to the police station where he was subjected to several hours of interrogation before being released. But the police weren't finished with Carlos yet. He was arrested a second time.

> *Secret police arrested him. His family had no idea where he was or even if he was alive.*

He recalls, "This time they tried to intimate my wife, telling her to prepare my bag because I would be in jail for a few days. They also confiscated my car, computer and printer, air conditioner, and some official church documents."

Carlos was released two days later, but with the ominous threat that they would see him again. As promised, five secret police arrested him on February 20, 2006. For a while, his family had no idea where he was or even if he was alive. Finally, he was moved into the Center for Crimes against the Security of the Cuban State. No charges were filed, no lawyer was permitted, and his family still had no contact with him.

At this point, I called several friends who minister to persecuted Christians. After hearing Carlos' story, they went into action. People from around the globe began interceding for Carlos and sending him cards and letters of encouragement. Christians, moved by God's compassion, responded in overwhelming numbers. Three, four, ten, and sometimes twenty letters a day began to arrive, telling Carlos people were praying for him. Uramis heard from the United States, Latin America, Belgium, and Mongolia. Every communication was encouragement and prayer support for the family. Carlos was amazed that Christians around the world cared so much about him.

"I was so tired," he recalls. "They fed us bad food, made us work hard, and tried to intimidate us every day. My blood pressure went up and I had daily headaches, but these letters gave me hope to hang on."

Carlos wasn't the only one who noticed the attention. Guards demanded that he tell people to stop writing, but Carlos responded, "I don't even know these people, but they are Christians who love me and are praying for me."

After Uramis discovered where Carlos was being held, they were allowed 10-minute family visits each Monday, always in the presence of guards. I e-mailed her every other day to encourage and remind her that God would deliver Carlos. I knew the power of prayer and that prayers from around the world would set him free.

On June 20, 2006, when Uramis went for her weekly visit, guards suddenly demanded, "Get your things and get out of here. We don't want you here anymore."

"Why?" a shocked Carlos asked. "You mean I can just go home?"

After 126 days in prison, Carlos was released, though not yet free. Court was scheduled for December 6, so another SOS for prayer was sent out. Again, by the hundreds, prayer warriors and intercessors moved into action. The first case that day was another pastor being tried on the same charge as Carlos—illegal trafficking of people out of Cuba. When asked if he had anything to say, he declined. With that, the case was closed and he was sentenced to nine years in prison.

Carlos and Uramis Lamelas with daughters Stephanie and Daniela

Yet I Will Rejoice

Next was Carlos. The same prosecutor also wanted nine years for him. Except for a miracle of God, the outcome was certain.

"Right before our eyes another miracle happened!" Carlos testifies. "The prosecutor suddenly got sick. God struck him with illness right there in the courtroom and he couldn't continue."

Another prosecutor was summoned, and another miracle took place. Amazingly, the new prosecutor acted more like a defense lawyer, arguing for acquittal because no crime had been committed. Carlos was declared not guilty, but he was still fined 1,000 Cuban pesos (about 40 U.S. dollars). Nevertheless, we were ecstatic for this was a battle that prayer had won.

After the trial, a Christian woman who'd testified against Carlos approached Uramis in tears, begged for forgiveness, and said her testimony had been coerced.

"Don't worry, sister," Uramis responded lovingly. "God has heard our prayer and we forgive you. Go in peace."

Unwavering Faith
by Cheryl Johnson Barton (Tokyo, Japan)

The young priest's conversion, although frowned upon, hadn't produced a tidal wave of opposition, at least not immediately. While he had been called to explain himself before an assembly of 100 top-level Buddhist sect heads who viewed him as an up-and-coming future leader, he had emerged from the ordeal stronger in his faith and all the more convinced that one day he would have the opportunity to share Christ even with these individuals.

Even when the heat was turned up and he had to leave the area for his own personal safety, the converted monk did not waver in his conviction. But the emotional strain began to take its toll on him physically. Perhaps a curse had been placed on him—not at all unheard of in that place. Losing nearly 30 pounds in one month, he could not eat or sleep and seemed in danger of losing his sanity. Still he declared, "I will not turn back. Truth is truth. One's circumstances—even difficult ones—do not change the truth."

LATIN AMERICA

After the hardest year of my life…

A Mouth Filled with Laughter

by Noily Hernández
(Las Vueltas, Costa Rica)

It is undeniable that God wants us to serve him with gladness (Psalm 100:2), but I wasn't always able to do that—not until recently.

I was 19 years old when God called me into the ministry. At the time, I was scared. I couldn't believe God would call a woman like me—the child of a poor, dysfunctional home, one who had suffered innumerable traumas, including sexual abuse. But God loved me, chose me, and called me to serve him anyway. Answering that call, I assisted my pastor for 10 years.

When the pastor resigned, the congregation named me lay leader. Later, in 1998, I became the official pastor. By then, I was married and had two daughters. My husband visited the church occasionally when everything was going well, but in reality, our family was in trouble. Still, I was willing to serve God even with my problems, and God always helped me. By January 2005, the Lord had blessed me spiritually in many ways. But I also knew great pain from my husband's abuse and unfaithfulness. My hardest test was when he betrayed me with my own mother.

On January 3, 2005, I was doing housework when suddenly I felt a stabbing pain in my heart. I was sure it was stress from all my difficulties. As on many other occasions, I raised my eyes to heaven and prayed, "God, help me!" And God responded to my cries.

"I had a vineyard," he told me. "I cleared it, took out the rocks, and waited for it to bear sweet grapes, but it only produced bitter ones. I ask, what more could I do for my vineyard that I have not already done?"

He continued, "Daughter, you have struggled for your marriage; you have forgiven your husband again and again. And so I ask you, what more could you do for him that you have not already done? Don't do anything more."

With that, I told my husband I wanted to separate and asked him to leave the house, but he pleaded for one more chance. So I made a covenant with God to wait one more year during which time I would pray and fast. It was the hardest year of my life, and I sought God like never before. I even went for professional help, but I was told that if my husband didn't want to change, I could do nothing. Things at home only got worse. When I thought I couldn't go on, I remembered my covenant.

Around October, on the third day of an extended fast, I faced a problem at home. When my husband discovered that I'd shared with my prayer team, he cursed me. Once again, I cried out to heaven. God instructed me to review my own heart. When I did, I was filled with a wonderful peace greater than all my problems.

I continued fasting and praying. On one especially difficult day, I went to church to talk to God there. I told him I felt like the Israelites under bondage in Egypt. God answered by personalizing Psalm 126:1–3: "When the Lord brought Noily out of captivity, she was like one in a dream. Her mouth was filled with laughter and her tongue with praise. Then they will say among the nations, 'The Lord has done great things for Noily, and she will be glad.'"

On January 3, 2006, my husband threatened me in front of our daughters. When my older daughter defended me, he struck her. When my younger daughter and I tried to intervene, he hit us too. Finally the day ended, but then the longest and most fearful night of my life began. My daughters and I were so afraid that we locked ourselves in a bedroom where I began crying. I had prayed earnestly for God to perform a miracle in my husband. It had not happened, and the covenant year was now over. I was disconsolate. Throughout the night, my husband kept pounding on the door, asking our forgiveness, but also justifying his actions.

Finally, my older daughter could stand it no longer. She asked me to sign a will giving her custody of her younger sister. It hurt to realize that the situation was so bad that she thought I might not live until morning. Painfully, I understood there were only two options: stay with my husband and end up in the cemetery or have the courage to declare my rights as a woman.

As the sun rose, I told my husband that the marriage was over, but he didn't believe me. Although I felt confused, I filed charges against him and asked him to leave the house, something that took the help of the police. When I was finally safe, I couldn't sleep. I spent the night praying, asking God why I'd had to endure everything. He comforted me, saying, "If I had not allowed this, you would never have left your slavery. When I brought Israel out of Egypt, their liberation was not easy, either."

That day God began to strengthen me and help me understand. Three days later, I returned to the church. My husband was there and I was afraid, but someone was always at my side to protect me as I spoke to the congregation, "We sing a praise song that says, 'A heart that praises God can't be sad,' but that isn't true. I'm very sad because I've made a very serious decision. Please respect it and pray for me."

After the service, I met with the church leaders and missionaries. Never before had I heard such words of support and encouragement. My pastoral team said they knew about my suffering, supported me fully, and wanted me to take a month of vacation. As I was going to get my daughters, I had a strange experience of laughter. While I began crying with relief, I also began laughing with happiness. My slavery was behind me!

A year has now passed since then. Finally, I am serving the Lord with gladness because he ended my suffering. Psalm 126 has come to pass in my life. The Lord freed me, filled my mouth with laughter, and gave me praise. Surely God has done great things in me.

Sharlin, Noily, and Sharom Hernández

The children's eyes haunted me.

Part of a Plan

by Jon Lambert
(Quito, Ecuador)

In 1992, I came to Ecuador on a work camp with my then 13-year-old son Mike. Taking a taxi to a shanty town outside Quito called Zabala, we visited a site where the young Ecuadorian church wanted to start a new congregation. We looked around the small lot and prayed about the possibilities of a new church in that dusty isolated place.

Then I saw them: the dirty baby girl in the tire swing and the little boy peering at us from behind a stack of discarded wooden cement forms. As I stared at their empty, haunting eyes, God spoke to the depths of my soul: "You will come back and you will help build a church here." They were not audible words but rather an intense realization, an impression stronger than words—a calling.

And the next year, I did return. The walls of the church building went up, only to be blown down by the largest dust devil I'd ever seen. As we worked, neighborhood children came to get candy and balloons and to play with the funny foreigners. Everyone crowded around us—except the two whose stares had drawn me back to Ecuador. They were always watching, but only from a distance.

A couple years later, I returned to Ecuador and the Zabala church. I looked for the two children and found them sitting on the front row of the sanctuary. As they sang in the program, my heart swelled to realize that obeying God's call had helped bring the hope of Jesus to those two children, Cristina and her brother Danny.

A few more years passed. My wife Karen and I were participating in a faith promise convention in Dewey, Oklahoma. Missionaries Jim and Mary Ann Hawkins were also there. One night, Jim asked me a question. "Why aren't you on the mission field?" I had a good answer, but Jim kept staring at me with a half smile. "You should be on the field," he said with certainty in his voice. My first response was to get angry.

Latin America

Jon Lambert, the "funny foreigner," still plays with Ecuadorian children today.

How can this crazy missionary know God's will for my life? I argued silently.

Once back in Hamilton, Ohio, I resumed my daily pastoral routine and tried to forget Jim's words about the "field." After all, I was working in a field, a nice big American field. But those children's eyes still haunted me. Then one morning in my office, God again moved on my heart. "Will you leave this ministry and go where I lead?" I couldn't evade his question.

We answered yes and moved to Ecuador in 1997. Years later, Karen and I were at the Zabala church again one Sunday morning. Danny, now 21, was sitting on the front row as before, but this time as a teacher. Looking at him, I was overjoyed with the realization that we had been part of bringing the gospel to a place where it had never been shared before. As a result, the life of this dynamic young man and his sister had been changed.

Yet I Will Rejoice

But as I looked more closely, I realized how tired, pale, and downcast Danny seemed. His alcoholic father had thrown him out of the house and he'd been sleeping on a neighbor's roof at night. This time the voice from heaven did not need to convince us. "Danny, you can stay with us," we responded.

Yesterday, Danny bounded into the kitchen for breakfast, his perpetual smile as bright as ever. He ate quickly and then flew out the door to a day of medical school classes and evening hospital rounds. Danny is one of the top medical students at his university. We had just put up family photos on a wall of our home the night before. There were many pictures of our kids. Danny beamed when he realized there was one of him too.

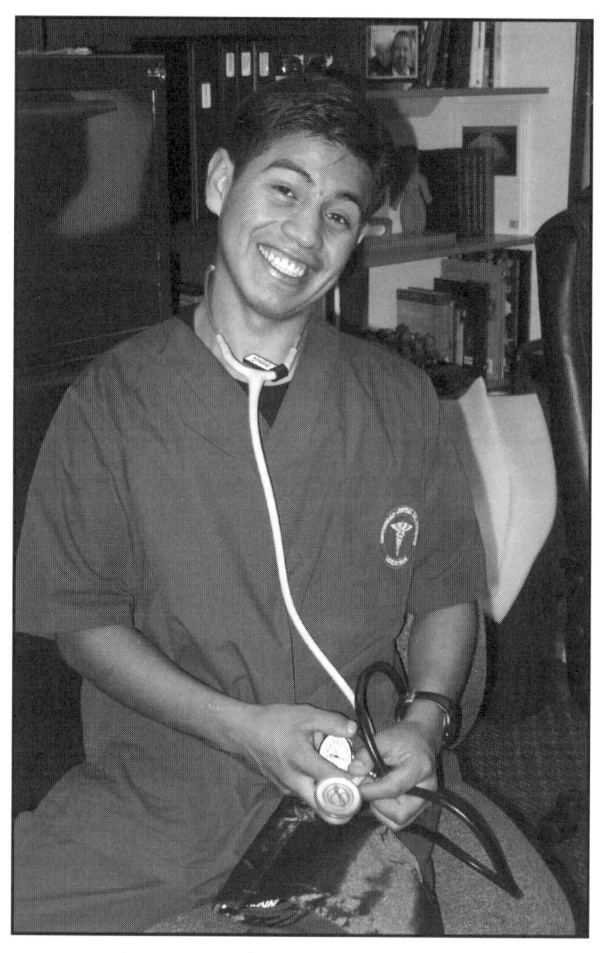

Dr. Danny—because missionaries came

"Brother Jon, if you hadn't come that day and returned to help us, I could never have become a doctor. I would be just like my father," he said appreciatively.

"For I know the plans I have for you," says God in Jeremiah 29:11. Indeed, God knew 14 years ago that Danny would need us today. He had a plan to call us to Ecuador for Danny and others. How exciting to be part of God's amazing plan that continues to unfold day after day.

When I felt completely helpless, God sent…

An Angel on Flight 3588

by Cheryl Johnson Barton
(Kobe, Japan)

I'd always believed in angels. Sort of. I guessed I had to believe in angels. They were in the Bible. But were they in my world? In honest moments, I wondered—until I traveled to Russia.

It was the spring of 1994 and I was on assignment for the Missionary Board.* The flight from Japan to Moscow had gone well, and I'd been met by my Russian host at the airport as scheduled. The next morning, Olek drove me to another airport for my flight to the city of Chelyabinsk. After he registered my ticket, I assured him I'd be fine and sent him on his way.

But it wasn't long before I realized I'd made a mistake. No signs or announcements were in English, and no one around spoke anything I understood. It was as if the lights had gone out and I was plunged into darkness. Not knowing what to expect, I could feel my anxiety rising. Eventually, I was driven to another building where, by trial and error, I got checked in. But no one took my bag or gave me a seat assignment. One woman motioned me up the stairs to a room with a few chairs, but little else. It was hard to believe I was really in an airport.

By that time, it was only an hour until my flight, and I still didn't know if I was in the right place. Whenever I tried to ask questions, I was met with bored expressions and the shrug of shoulders. Feeling utterly helpless, I sat tentatively in a chair and stared at the wall before me. It was covered with stickers, most of which I couldn't read. However, one jumped out at me from the jumbled mess: "God Listens." Helpless? Yes. But alone, no. My spirits lifted a bit.

Eventually a man approached. When he spoke to me in English, I felt like I'd been rescued. I told him where I was going, and he said my flight

---
* Now called Global Missions.

Yet I Will Rejoice

Flying to Chelyabinsk (right), where today a Church of God building (below) is under construction

had already been announced. I almost panicked until my eyes fell upon that sign again. God was with me.

"They're calling you," he told me when a woman appeared and announced something I didn't understand. He stood, picked up my bag, and declared, "I'll go with you to make sure you get through okay."

Relief must have been written all over my face. It lasted through the final check and as I climbed the steps to the waiting plane, but I was in for a shock at the top. The cabin was crammed beyond capacity. There was no place for me to sit, no hope of stowing my bags, and I had no seat assignment.

After pushing halfway into the cabin, I noticed a very distinguished-looking man standing at the entrance to a row of seats. He caught my eye and motioned me to come. It was only then I noticed the two empty seats in his row. With him standing and looking back, I thought he was searching for his traveling companions—the ones for whom he'd held the seats. Instead, he grabbed my maroon bag and wrestled it to the floor in front of the window seat. Still wearing my bulging backpack, I squeezed into my seat, my feet straddling my bag on the floor. Somehow I got my backpack into my lap from a seated position.

As I sat there, the gentleman motioned me to put my backpack on the floor in front of the middle seat. But where, I wondered, will that person put his feet? Suddenly I realized there would be no other person. Those two seats had been saved just for my bags and me. From that moment, I thought of this companion as my gentleman angel.

God had commanded a gentleman angel.

After landing in Chelyabinsk, I was wondering how to extract my things from between the cramped seats when my gentleman angel pulled my backpack up and handed it to me. Then grabbing my suitcase, he headed down the aisle quickly and was on the waiting bus outside on the tarmac before I even reached the aisle. When I found him, he'd saved a place for me to stand beside my suitcase that he'd shouldered.

Although the bus was crowded, I managed to glimpse the terminal through the window and breathed a sigh of relief. I'd made it! When I turned my head back to thank the gentleman for his kindness, he was nowhere to be seen. The bus was still packed, and he couldn't have moved three inches, but he was gone. I never saw him again.

I no longer doubt angels. "For he will command his angels concerning you to guard you in all your ways," reads Psalm 91:11. In my case, God had commanded a gentleman angel.

Yet I Will Rejoice

UPDATE

When Cheryl Johnson Barton first wrote this story for *In the Shadow of Your Wings* (1997), she and her husband Bernie had been pastoring a Japanese congregation in Kobe, Japan, for nearly 15 years. One year later, Bernie became principal of Tamagawa Seigakuin, a girls junior and senior high school in Tokyo. This led to completing their pastoral assignment in 2003 and moving to Tokyo. The Kobe church remains without a pastor today, Bernie continues as principal, and Cheryl is involved in discipling and writing ministries.

Many things also have changed in Chelyabinsk. In 1994, the year of this story, Kelley and Rhonda Philips were founding pastors of the fledgling Church of God there and were working hard to develop national leadership both in the city and the nation. Today the congregation of 200 people is pastored by Sergei Sokol and Andrei Kolegov. Happy news from the Chelyabinsk church is its soon-to-be-completed building project and its outreach to prison inmates, with special emphasis on those who are HIV positive.

The Philipses now live in Berlin, Germany. They have been regional coordinators for the Europe–Middle East region since 2002.

Following the Lord in baptism in Russia

The signs of God's presence are unmistakable. They are seen in…

THE FINGERPRINTS OF GOD

BHUTAN

Bhutan is a predominantly Buddhist country that begins where the Himalayan Mountains begin to break out of the northeast appendage of the subcontinent of India. It is here, along the rather porous border between India and Bhutan, that I met Pastor Simon Chaudrey (not his real name), his son, and a group of coworkers who evangelize along the border. Pastor Simon is in his mid-seventies, I suppose, but is still very active in ministry.

"At times this is a very dangerous place to live," Pastor Simon said, pointing in the direction of a rather unproductive plot of land where maize was growing. "We always say that half the crop is for us and half is for the elephants that rampage through here. At times our neighbors are killed by the elephants."

But this is not the only danger of living and ministering in this area. On a regular basis, at least during the six months when the rains have stopped and he can cross the river and climb the seemingly vertical walls of Bhutan that rise up just a kilometer or so inside the border, Pastor Simon leads a ministry to the people of Bhutan, a nation closed to all Christian witness until 1965. Presently there are two congregations there.

"The people, although Buddhist, are animists," Pastor Simon said, explaining how they are held captive to the world of spirits and demons. When trouble comes, they depend on religious practitioners to determine the spiritual reasons for the problems and then devise the appropriate sacrifice to appease the offended spirits.

"The best way that the gospel is introduced is through healings," the elderly pastor shared. "There are many people who are sick and can't be healed through witchcraft. So we tell them that Jesus can heal them. Some of the most effective scriptures for us to use are those where Jesus is casting out the evil spirits."

Yet I Will Rejoice

Speaking about their methods of sharing the Good News in this area, he continued, "We have five pastors and evangelists working in this border area. This gives them the freedom to work either in India or Bhutan."

We were introduced to several coworkers. One pastor travels regularly into Bhutan, despite the fact that the police there are always on the lookout for him because he has led many away from Buddhism and their folk beliefs of animism. Many have come to Christ as a result of the ministry of this pastor and his wife.

An evangelist in India, on the Bhutan border

This pastor also has a healing ministry. In one case, he related that a village leader in Bhutan was very sick. Various witchdoctors had tried all types of magic on him, but nothing worked. When the pastor heard about this village leader, he went to pray for him and the man (we would say "miraculously," he would say "naturally") was healed in a couple of hours. Afterwards, the village leader began to testify to all. Angry villagers quickly surrounded the pastor. His defense? "I am not trying to teach bad things." Then, pointing to the man who was healed, he continued, "I am trying to bring good things to the people of Bhutan."

"After that," the pastor finished his story, "the group dispersed and left me alone."

Please pray for Pastor Simon Chaudrey and the other pastors and evangelists living and working on the Bhutan border. Pray that they will be encouraged and strengthened in their daily fight against the forces of evil and darkness.

—**John M. Johnson**
Portland, Oregon

POTPOURRI

CAMBODIA

Our trip to Cambodia in the summer of 2007 was very memorable because we were invited to visit a prison in Phnom Penh. There we heard wonderful news of what God is doing among the prisoners.

About six years ago, a woman in Singapore bought a copy of Neville's

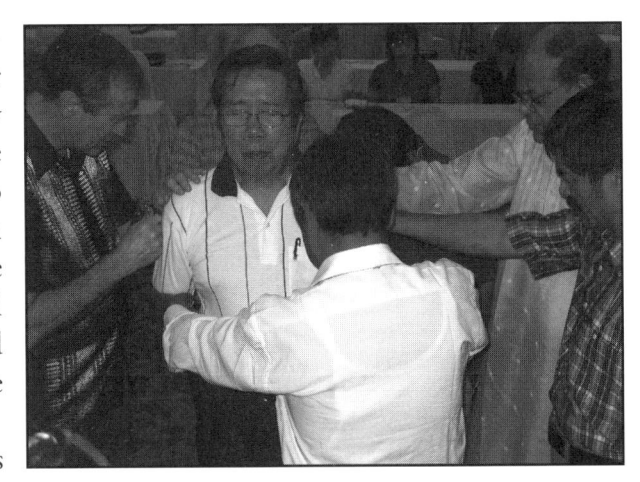

Asian church leaders pray for healing for Neville Tan (center, with glasses).

autobiography, *Iron Man*, and sent it to her brother serving a 20-year prison term in Cambodia for drug offenses. The book was passed to another prisoner who was doing time for kidnapping. Although he'd become a Christian, he was feeling very discouraged. Reading *Iron Man* gave him hope and inspiration, and God used him to share Neville's book with others.

A couple of years later, he and a few others who'd received Christ in prison decided to translate the book into the Khmer language. Korean missionaries who run a Bible school in Cambodia helped raise the necessary funds. Through a donor in Singapore, 2,000 copies of the book were printed for distribution to prisoners and for sale in Cambodia.

It was wonderful to be able to visit this man and his friends in prison and discover the fantastic ministry they have there. About a third of the inmates—50 out of 150—have come to know Christ. This brother was to have been release d in May, shortly before our visit, but his release papers still hadn't arrived. Words cannot describe our joy when, as we were speaking to the prisoners, it was announced that his papers had come through. That same afternoon, we were able to have lunch with him. He still has a burden for his friends who remain in prison and is praying to make *Iron Man* available to every inmate in all of Cambodia's prisons. For a start, we have committed the proceeds of 500 copies of our English and Chinese versions in order to reprint another 2,000 copies in Khmer for distribution in the prisons.

—**Neville and Anne Tan**
Singapore

CENTRAL ASIA

It didn't take long at the tea house for the police to show up. We'd had only two meetings there, but somebody complained to the landlord and the police. The tea house manager, a seeker, had to suffer the brunt. Another man faced harassment and threats last summer when he helped an outreach team gather a crowd of several hundred people. It's a difficult country, and it's hard to watch my friends suffer—and they aren't even believers yet! Imagine how much harder it would be if they became believers. But that's the point of the persecution, to halt their move toward the gospel.

Despite this trouble, the tea house manager introduced me this week to

Tea house country scenery

a smooth businessman who interrogated me in a friendly way. He often goes to the tea house in the mornings. One day he overheard some men there talking about our meetings. I don't think he has spiritual interest exactly, but he was curious. He wanted to tell me that I'll never be able to change these "hard-headed" Muslims (his words, not mine). I replied that I can't change anybody, and then I told him the parable of the pearl of great price. I want to keep telling that parable so my friends will consider that the kingdom of God is worth all the hardship they will face. I also told him that God placed a love in my heart for the people of Central Asia, and I want to bless them. I don't know how much sank in, but I'm praying that God will open his eyes to the truth.

We still have 70 names of people from the Bible correspondence course who live in our general vicinity. Please pray for us as we contact them to sit down, have some tea together, and get acquainted. Many of these people are genuinely open spiritually. But the biggest challenge we are facing is where and how to gather them together because of social and political obstacles. May the Lord turn around the "tea house trouble" for his glory.

—**A Church of God missionary**

CHINA

I'd arrived at the house of my host at midnight after a 12-hour bus ride. I had a good rest and a wonderful Mongolian breakfast. Local co-workers came to the house one by one after they received the message that I'd arrived. We were so happy to see each other after more than a year, and they gave me a warm welcome. We talked and talked, sharing what had happened during the year, and I was giving a message for them from Genesis 50:15–21.

A Chinese woman awaits the gospel.

Suddenly, someone was knocking on the door. My host asked me to hide in another room. I did, just before the deputy chief of the Religious Affairs Bureau and his assistant came into the living room. My host treated them politely as they questioned him. A few minutes later, they entered the room where our co-workers were and shouted at them. I was there, too, right behind the door. Amazingly, I was completely calm, for the Lord was with me. I was ready to face the official if he looked behind the door, but he did not.

Satisfied for the moment, the two officers went back to the living room, but they sternly announced to the host, "We have information that Pastor L will come to your house during these two days. When he comes, you must let us know. We want to talk to him." The host replied wisely and they left. We were all surprised and wondered how they had the information.

Changing my plans, I waved farewell to my co-workers after dinner. As I left the city, I prayed for God's protection over the church, asking him to keep the believers strong in their difficult and dangerous situation. I knew he had protected me too.

—A Church of God pastor

ECUADOR

Some years ago, Pastor Jorge Arroba was asked to visit a partially paralyzed, bitter old man. He lived in a bamboo shack several blocks from the Quevedo church. Pastor Arroba shared the gospel with him, and he immediately accepted Christ as his Savior. Since then, Brother Akario has been a faithful follower of Jesus and almost never misses a service.

On our recent visit to Quevedo, we arrived at the church a bit early for a midweek service. There

Pastor Jorge Arroba and wife

in the darkness stood 89-year-old Brother Akario, all alone and leaning on his cane. Wet, tired, and weak, he was out of breath and wheezing.

"How did you get here, brother?" I asked, greeting him.

"I walked," he answered with a half grin. It was then almost seven o'clock.

"How long did it take you?" I continued my questions.

"I left my house at 4:30," he replied.

Incredibly, Brother Akario had fought a five-block battle for more than two hours. Dragging his paralyzed side, leaning unsteadily on a crude cane, and moving through a drizzling rain, he had come to church.

After service, we took Brother Akario to his house, a seven-minute drive by car. As we helped him inside, we noticed that it was leaning precariously. The wooden beam supports had rotted away and the little shanty was falling in. We looked around to see a rough chair, a modest single bed that was damp because of holes in the roof, a few dishes, and nothing more.

We couldn't help but wonder what in Brother Akario's life would motivate such devotion to God. His wife is dead, his health is poor, his house is falling in, and he has no means of making a living. But he has found a treasure greater than health or financial security—eternal life in Jesus Christ. We decided to rebuild his house. He was grateful, but he insisted that there are many others with greater needs than his.

—**Jon and Karen Lambert**
Quito, Ecuador

KENYA

In March 2007, I planned a trip to Tanzania to see two Kima International School of Theology (KIST) students on their internships. (All third-year students have a three-month internship.) It was a five-hour drive to the border of Kenya and Tanzania. After dealing with two offices on the Kenya side of the border, I entered Tanzania, but getting my car into Tanzania was another story altogether. I had to go to seven different offices where people manually logged my car information, checked what the others had done, relogged information, rechecked, checked again, and finally, after an hour, approved my automobile to travel in Tanzania.

After another hour of driving, we arrived at Mennonite Theological College on the Tanzanian side of Lake Victoria, a beautiful location. It is the only Mennonite training center in East Africa. Their students

Yet I Will Rejoice

can earn either a certificate or a diploma; those who want to advance further usually come to KIST.

It was wonderful to see our two students, both of whom were teaching at the college for their internships. I proudly visited their classes and found them doing a great job. Students often call me Mom, and I feel as proud of them as any mother could.

Rebecca Pierce visits student teachers.

Talking with my students, I realized that, except for the principal, the teaching staff there all graduated from KIST. It was even more exciting for me to know that I'd taught all of those graduates at one time or another. How cool to see the products of your work and know they are passing on what they learned to others.

There is a saying in Africa: "Christianity is a mile wide but an inch deep." In other words, people are receptive to the gospel but do not grow deeply in their faith. Praise God that theological training is helping to change this. As the more than 100 KIST graduates from five African nations learn and then teach others, they are having a huge impact on the continent. KIST just graduated 34 students, and I am waiting to see how God uses them. Graduates are teaching, preaching, working in community projects, and even leading general assemblies. Praise God!

—**Rebecca Pierce**
Kima, Kenya

SINGAPORE

Singapore is a strikingly affluent city. Signs of wealth are everywhere. There are huge modern buildings downtown. We've seen Lamborghinis

Potpourri

and Rolls Royces, even though cars cost double the U.S. price. Everyone walks around with cell phones and MP3 players. What's happening in the U.S. stock market leads off each day's local news. There is a preoccupation with wealth.

I have to admit I've been consumed with money over the past few months as well.

Jeff Ingram on the Singapore coast

When we agreed to come to Singapore, I knew we'd need more funds. Because the Asia–Pacific region is a new field for HCJB Global, our support schedule had to be developed, then reworked, and then reworked again. Each time, my heart stopped as we learned we needed to raise $1,000, then $1,500, and then $2,000 more per month.

The closer we got to our departure date, the more I worried, fretted, sighed, and panicked. I worked, pushed, pleaded, and recrunched numbers. What I didn't do was display a lot of faith. But in spite of me, God has been faithful. Through the first five months of this year, we were averaging $2,000 less a month than we needed to move. Over the past four months, we've been fully supported.

I'll tell you, though, even as funds increased, my faith struggled. After June's statement, Nancy said, "Yippee!" I said, "There are lots of one-time gifts here. Next month we won't have them." July's statement came, and the conversation was repeated. August was the single largest month we've had in years. September was another fully supported month, and I'm finally writing this. How can I not be encouraged and thankful? The generosity of God's people has been breathtaking.

This has been a great reminder to me that God is faithful even in my faithlessness. Even when I can't muster the courage to say, "I know he'll take care of this," he takes care of it anyway.

—**Jeff Ingram**
Singapore

Yet I Will Rejoice

SOUTHEAST ASIA

It was early Monday morning when I left the house to go jogging on the high school track, and it was just starting to get light when I began walking home.

My headphones were out of my ears as I walked, and there was already plenty of traffic on the road. But as I neared the corner to turn into our neighborhood, I heard a motorbike behind me and had a strange premonition, a feeling that extra caution was needed. I started clenching my fist as I walked. I wasn't sure if the motorbike would turn in behind me, but it did, and its lights were off. As I turned to look, it was right by my leg and its rider, a man, tried to grab me. I must have pulled back from him and swung (no contact), and then I yelled.

At my shout, he drove away. I saw his brake lights come on and was afraid he would return, so I hid behind some banana trees, trying to catch up with my racing heart. When I saw some other folks jog by, I started the short distance back home again, sobbing the whole way.

Today as I walked home from school, I found myself turning to look at each bike before it got to me, even in broad daylight. I don't particularly think I was in extreme danger Monday morning. I think the man was taking advantage of a situation with a woman, a white woman at that. But it certainly didn't feel that way then.

Since then, I have contemplated the presence of God in that situation. I took my headphones out (which I do not always do) and was able to hear the motorbike approaching. God gave me a feeling that something was amiss and I was able to react much faster than I might have otherwise. As I hugged Casey after getting home, he said that at the time of the incident, he was awake because of our son and was praying for safety for our entire family. As a result, I was not hurt, just a little traumatized.

Prayers for us are such a blessing! God's protection and provision are very real too.

—**Sharon Bernhardt**
Southeast Asia

TANZANIA

One of the blessings of preparing to move to Tanzania in 2006 was visiting the Women of the Church of God (WCG) Linen Chest. We'd heard of it before but had no idea what an incredible gift WCG gives to missionaries. The Linen Chest is a large room in the WCG office that has floor-to-ceiling shelves filled with brand-new bedding, towels, and kitchen supplies for us to choose from to take to the field. We were able to stock our entire home with linens and supplies for our bedrooms, bathrooms, and kitchen.

A little girl in rural Tanzania

We were running late for an appointment in Cincinnati, so Mike started packing up the car while I made our final selections. The item that caught my attention most was a set of measuring cups and spoons on the bottom shelf. Just the week before, I was spending a Christmas gift card and contemplating buying a new set of measuring cups. Standing in the store, I picked them up off the shelf and put them back numerous times, finally deciding I didn't really need them. I rationalized that there were probably measuring cups in our house in Tanzania, and even though I'd really like to take a new set, I could get by with the ones already there. But there on the bottom shelf at the Linen Chest was a whole set of matching (I love matching) measuring cups and spoons. They were similar to the ones I'd looked at in the store, only these were better and nicer.

I was struck by God's loving care of me, his attention to the details of my life, and how he knew that a really nice set of matching measuring cups and spoons would make my day and remind me of him. We left the Linen Chest feeling overwhelmed by God's goodness and provision.

—**Heather Webb**
Dodoma, Tanzania

BEHIND THE SCENES

WHETHER I LIVE OR DIE (page 6)—West Africa Bible Institute (IBAO), where the author of this story is preparing for ministry, was launched in January 2007 with 14 students, half of whom were already pastors. Courses are held during two-week intensive modules conducted every two months, allowing students to continue working and caring for their families while studying. Teachers include missionaries Sherman and Kay Critser and LeAnn and Larry Sellers, who translated this story from French. IBAO is the first French-speaking Bible institute of the Church of God in the world.

Larry and LeAnn Sellers

WHY I SERVE IN UGANDA (page 9)—A Canadian missionary nurse since October 2004, Glenna Phippen is healthcare facilitator of the medical department of the Church of God in Uganda. As such, she oversees the operations of four clinics and helps promote public health education. "I'm still in awe of how the Lord provides what we need, and always on time," she said at the start of her second term in 2007. She reports that Eveline retains use of her scarred hands and started school a few months after her accident.

Glenna Phippen

PRAISE IN A BARREN FIELD and **THE FINGERPRINTS OF GOD** (pages 12, 87)—After teaching at a Christian school during two years as special assignment missionaries in Southeast Asia, Heather and Mike Webb became career missionaries to Tanzania in 2006. They address holis-

Potpourri

tic health needs by teaching spiritual principles, preventative health practices, and appropriate technology in a program called CHE (Community Health Evangelism). In it, a small group of villagers is empowered to teach what they've learned to others so the entire community benefits.

Mike and Heather Webb

THE RAVAGER (page 14)—Missionary Kay Critser reports that although Valy died March 2, 2008, he lived a year longer than predicted and used his time to testify to God's goodness in many churches. "We just lost a pastor's wife to AIDS, which she contracted from her first husband," Kay shares, adding that the pastor is now positive too. "I've also just learned of another church leader who has the virus, contracted during one moment of knowing a man about five years ago. That's about the time it takes for the virus to show itself, and death is usually within 10 years. We have an epidemic on our hands, even in the church."

Sherman and Kay Critser

A RADICAL STORY (page 17)—Missionary Bernie Barton, who translated this testimony from Japanese into English, had the joy of baptizing Eriko Tanaka at Hagiyama Church of God on July 15, 2007. Tanaka-san is the mother of a third-grade daughter who lives with her former husband and his family. Since her radical conversion, Tanaka-san is in contact with them once again and prays daily that God will restore her family even as he restored her life.

Bernie Barton

Yet I Will Rejoice

THE RASCAL OF MANDALAY and **THE FINGERPRINTS OF GOD** (pages 20, 77)—At the time of these stories, John and Gwen Johnson were regional coordinators for Global Missions of Church of God Ministries in the Asia–Pacific region. Although John now teaches at Warner Pacific College, Portland, Oregon, he remains passionate about missions and is enthusiastic about the school's new Christian missions minor. Meeting Kyaw Thi Ha and his wife at a training conference recently, John recalls, "By their smiles alone, one could tell that their faith was genuine and that their love for each other and God has grown even deeper."

John and Gwen Johnson

BABY SAMMY and **THE FINGERPRINTS OF GOD** (pages 23, 86)—Long before Sharon and Casey Bernhardt became special assignment missionaries in 1998, Sharon knew the mission field, having grown up in Thailand as the daughter of missionaries. Now she and Casey are raising their own two sons, Ryan (age 6) and Niko (age 4), abroad as they serve on the faculty and staff of a Christian international school where many students are themselves missionary kids. Of Sammy, Sharon reports that he turned one in October 2007 and is "absolutely beautiful."

Casey, Ryan, Niko, and Sharon Bernhardt

LESSONS FROM THE TSUNAMI (page 26)—Leaderwell Pohsngap served from 1994 to 2007 on the governing board of World Vision India. Formerly a Church of God pastor and president of Union Biblical Seminary in Pune, India, he is an international director of Global

POTPOURRI

Leaderwell and Rivulet Pohsngap

LEAD Alliance, facilitating local churches in leadership development. With his wife Rivulet, he worked under the Mission Board of the Church of God in Meghalaya/Assam (India) as a teacher at Kima International School of Theology (KIST) in Kenya from 1981 to 1983.

A NEW WAY FORWARD (page 29)—God healed Song Cheng Hock of bipolar disorder at just the right time—just when the Church of God in Singapore and its founding pastor, Neville Tan, needed an interim in 2006. Since then, Song has assumed that pastorate full-time, allowing Neville and his wife Anne to give their full attention to evangelism and missions work in Southeast Asia. Pastor Song and his wife Nellie have been married for 27 years and are the parents of four children: Ben, Joy, Mark, and Luke.

Pastor Song and Joy

OUTSIDE THE GARDEN OF EDEN (page 32)—John Ackerman has been a medical missionary in Haiti since 1986. He is married to Jodie, whose missionary assignments include teaching kindergarten at an international school in the capital city of Port-au-Prince. A registered nurse, John conducts three weekly clinics in the remote village of Prospere, in the downstairs of the church pastored by Espasian Francois, Eden's father. Eden, 35 years old, is the mother of two children, 9 and 13.

Jodie, Jessica, and John Ackerman

Yet I Will Rejoice

I AM NOT ALONE (page 35)—The author of this moving testimony of God's sustaining presence has requested anonymity because of the sensitivity of the issues that have resulted in significant personal stress and strained relationships both within the national church and between associated regional and international bodies. Please pray for the more than 80 missionaries deployed by Church of God Ministries around the globe. Many of these persons carry very heavy loads and serve in extremely difficult locations.

UNDER A MANGO TREE (page 37)—When Kelvin Harrinarine thanks God for his blessings, he always remembers West Indies Theological College, the leadership training school from which he and 217 students have graduated since its founding in 1950. In 2007, 40 students from many of the Caribbean islands, including Trinidad and Tobago, Antigua, Barbados, St. Kitts, and Grenada were training there under such teachers as JoAnn Tate, a special assignment missionary, along with her husband Bob, since 2007.

JoAnn and Bob Tate

THINGS YOU THINK BUT NEVER SAY (page 39)—After 21 years of missionary work in Haiti, Phil and Lonnie Murphy returned to the United States in 2007. They have relocated to Florida, although they continue to be involved with Haiti through organizing work teams, co-ordinating and conducting a summer camp for underprivileged children, and raising money for House of Blessings Orphanage, directed by Tania and Franky Desir, whose daughter Fabbie was kidnapped and released early in 2007.

Lonnie and Phil Murphy and their "grandchildren"

Potpourri

A CHRISTMAS PERSPECTIVE (page 43)—Missionaries since 2005, David and Kathy Simpson were overwhelmed by the loving response of the Church of God in Plodiv in gathering more used clothes and more than enough new socks for the children. Consequently, the home's director invited the church to provide "moral teaching" to the children. Since then, even though the home is nearly 45 miles away, the congregation has been visiting regularly and ministering to both spiritual and physical needs.

Kathy Simpson and Bulgarian church women

IN THE SHEPHERD'S ARMS (page 46)—At the time of Klara's accident, Hans-Ulrich Linke pastored the Church of God in Haiterbach, Germany. Today Richard and Metta Baumgartner lead the congregation and report that Klara "is a wise woman when it comes to spiritual issues and a powerful worker when practical things are to be done in the church," including driving a car to bring others to church whenever possible. The church in Haiterbach is one of 26 Church of God congregations in Germany.

Metta and Richard Baumgartner

MIRACLE IN FLORENCE (page 49)—Because the author is building relationships in a nation that restricts religious freedoms and periodically expels foreigners for engaging in ministry while involved in secular professions, Susan English's true identity and Flora's birth name cannot be given. Please pray for the persecuted church around the world.

93

Yet I Will Rejoice

SWEET GRANDMA MARY (page 51)—Author Lena Barannikova is the women's leader at the Chelyabinsk Church of God, where Grandma Mary was active from 1997 until her death in 2006. Her daughter, with whom she lived, "is showing some interest in the church, God, and faith." Lena asks for prayer for Galina to come to Christ and for the church's building project. Prices in Russia have tripled since construction began, nearly halting the project and severely taxing the church, planted by Kelley and Rhonda Philips.

Rhonda and Lena

I WILL STAND AND WATCH (page 53)—In addition to serving as academic dean of Mediterranean Bible College, Don Deena Johnson enjoys preaching and worshiping in various churches in Lebanon, including the Church of God in Antilias, the vibrant group she introduced in this story. Planted by an Egyptian theological student in 2002, the church birthed a second congregation in West Beirut in 2007 and is now making plans to launch a third one. Pastor Jemima has lived in Lebanon for eight years.

Jemima and Don Deena

THE STRONG ARMS OF CHRIST (page 56)—Paul and Brenda Maxfield became directors of Children of Promise, the Church of God child sponsorship program, in 2003 after serving 13 years as special assignment missionaries (SAMs)

Paul and Brenda Maxfield

POTPOURRI

in the Cayman Islands and Costa Rica. Brenda resigned this position in 2007 to return to teaching but still accompanies Paul occasionally on visits to the 3,100-plus children sponsored by Children of Promise in 21 countries, including Ghana, Myanmar, Tanzania, and the Philippines.

SOUTH AMERICA ON MY HEART (page 60)—Fritz Killisch was a German missionary to Argentina from 1960 to 1964. During this time, he started the first Bible training school for Church of God ministers there. Picking up the vision, his concert-violinist-turned-missionary grandson Manuel graduated from seminary in 2007 and now serves the church in Argentina as it recovers from several devastating years and looks to the future through preparing a new generation of leaders.

Manuel Killisch

THE BATTLE THAT PRAYER WON (page 63)—Luz Gonzales, a retired pastor, continues his work as evangelist and mentor in many different Spanish-speaking locations. Of Carlos, he says, "Although he was found innocent, he is forbidden to pastor now or work in a government-approved job. This means he must support his family however he can. We praise God who faithfully provides each day's needs." In 2007, there were 3,300 constituents in the 89 Churches of God in Cuba.

Carol and Luz Gonzales

A MOUTH FILLED WITH LAUGHTER (page 67)—One of the last things Kathi Sellers did before leaving Costa Rica in July 2007 was to translate this story from Spanish into English. Then she returned to

Yet I Will Rejoice

Kathi and Wayne Sellers

packing boxes and the difficult task of saying good-bye to Costa Rica and Nicaragua after more than 15 years of joint missionary work there with her husband Wayne. Pastor Noily remains in Costa Rica, serving God faithfully in the church and as mother to Sharom (age 18) and Sharlin (age 12).

PART OF A PLAN and **THE FINGERPRINTS OF GOD** (pages 70, 82)—The Lamberts share exciting news of the launch of another new congregation in Ecuador: "In March 2007, Brother Lema attended a funeral where people were talking about death and its hopelessness. He began to share his hope in Jesus and invited everyone to his home to talk further. More than 20 neighbors crowded into his home the next week. Brother Lema, who doesn't consider himself a preacher, shared a message and asked if anyone wanted to accept Jesus Christ as their Savior. The entire group stood, and the San Martin Church of God was born."

Jon and Karen Lambert with Danny

THE FINGERPRINTS OF GOD

- **Neville and Anne Tan**, of Singapore, are regional evangelists in Southeast Asia. (page 79)
- The missionary who wrote from Central Asia and the pastor who wrote from China cannot be named because of security risks in the countries where they serve. (pages 80, 81)
- **Rebecca Pierce** has served at Kima International School of Theology since 2003. (page 83)
- Before relocating to Singapore in 2007, **Jeff Ingram** and his family were special assignment missionaries (SAMs) with HCJB Global in Ecuador. (page 84)